Blueberry Hill

Grandma's Best Recipes

This edition published in 2011.

Parragon
Queen Street House
4 Queen Street
Bath
BA1 1HE, UK

ISBN: 978-1-4454-4053-8

Printed in China

Notes for the reader:

All spoon measurements are level.

Unless otherwise stated milk is assumed to be whole and eggs are medium-size.

Times given are an approximate guide only. Preparation times differ according to different techniques used by different people and the cooking times may also vary from those given as a result of the type of oven used.

Sufferers from nut allergies should be aware that some of the ready-prepared ingredients used in the recipes in this book may contain nuts. Always check the packaging before use.

Recipes using raw or very lightly cooked eggs should be avoided by infants, the elderly, pregnant women, convalescents, and anyone with a chronic condition.

Contents

Welcome to Blueberry Hill

The kitchen is the heart of the home, and for many, Grandma was the heart of the kitchen. Even if we didn't have a grandmother who created delicious culinary memories for us, we yearn for those scrumptious foods that evoke happy remembrances of home cooking. You'll find those dishes—and those memories—in *Grandma's Best Recipes*.

Whether Grandma came from Ireland two centuries ago, Italy two generations ago, or Mexico two decades ago, the recipes featured in *Grandma's Best Recipes* express the highest quality of home cooking from a broad range of ethnic and regional origins.

Blueberry Hill Books are produced by a consortium of top-notch cooks and food professionals who have created a collection of hundreds of delectable family-style recipes, from appetizers to desserts. Each and every dish has been carefully tested, assuring perfect results every time.

Whether you consider yourself a gourmet or a beginning cook we're sure that our books will soon become a well-used collection on your shelf. In Grandma's Best Recipes, you'll find a diverse and delicious range of 130 recipes ranging from Grandma's breakfast dishes through to family meals and bake sale treats.

Here's to Grandma's everywhere.

Blueberry Hill

Pantry Essentials

A well-stocked pantry helps to make life a little easier when trying to plan out what to cook. The ingredients listed below are the things you'll regularly find on our shopping list.

Dry Ingredients

Pasta Spaghetti and macaroni are good basic pastas but for a broader choice add lasagna (sheets), Cannelloni (tubes), fusilli (spirals), farfalle (bows), tagliatelle (ribbons) and conchiglie (shells).

Rice Every pantry should have a good long-grain rice supplemented with basmati rice, risotto rice and brown rice.

Noodles Most noodles are associated with Asian cooking. Make sure you have a selection of both Egg noodles and rice noodles for use in soups and stir-fries.

Flour All-purpose flour is great for thickening casseroles, making sauces and coating food before cooking. Self-rising flour is used for baking whilst bread making generally requires specific bread flour due to higher gluten levels.

Sugar White and brown sugar cover off the basic needs, but some recipes will call for confectioner's sugar for making frostings and for decoration.

Nuts and Seeds Walnuts, almonds, pine nuts and cashews can be used to add extra crunch and texture to savory dishes and baked goods. Make sure to store them in airtight containers. Sesame seeds are useful for many Asian inspired dishes.

Oils & Vinegars

Extra Virgin Olive Oil Ideal for drizzling over salads Extra Virgin Olive Oil is produced from the first cold-pressing of the olives and is a premium olive oil with a peppery, fruity flavor.

Vegetable Oil Made of a blend of various oils this is best used for frying, as it is very greasy.

Peanut Oil Suitable for drizzling, dressings and mayonnaise as well as forms of cooking this is a very versatile oil.

Wine Vinegars Available in many different varieties, mainly red, white and sherry. They can be used for dressings, marinades, and sauces or sprinkled over foods.

Balsamic Vinegar This delicious vinegar is thick, dark and slightly sweet. It is made from grape juice that is aged in barrels over a number of years.

Herbs & Spices

Nothing beats fresh herbs or spices but it's always good to have the following dried herbs and spices to hand.

Chili Powder This powdered mixture of spices includes dried chiles, cumin, coriander and cloves. Use it to flavor soups and stews.

Paprika This spice is made from ground sweet red pepper pods and its flavor can vary from mild, sweet and pungent to fiery hot. It is excellent in salad and as a garnish.

Bay Leaves Originally from the Mediterranean dried bay leaves add a good pungent flavor to soups, sauces and casseroles. They are usually discarded once the food has absorbed their flavor.

Chives Relatives of the onion family these herbs can be added to salads, soups, cream cheese and egg dishes.

Garlic A must for any kitchen fresh cloves of garlic store well or you can buy jars of garlic cloves or dried garlic for your dishes.

Thyme A very versatile herb that can be used with meat, poultry, egg and potato dishes and is also good in soups, sauces, roasts, casseroles and stews.

Five Spice Chinese five spice seasoning is a blend of cloves, cinnamon, fennel seeds, Sichuan peppercorns and Star Anise. It is very popular in stir-fries.

Ginger Dried ginger is particularly good with fruit, cookies and condiments.

Apple Pie Spice This blend of spices usually consists of cinnamon, nutmeg and cardamom. It has a warm, sweet flavor and is delicious in fruit desserts, bread, cakes cookies, pies and drinks.

Other Items

Bouillon Cubes Great for use in casseroles and soups if you do not have time to make or buy fresh stock.

Tomato Paste This is a condensed puree, which adds a more intense flavor in sauces and soups.

Canned Tomatoes Always useful for a variety of dishes, from sauces and soups to stews and casseroles.

Canned Beans Always have a few cans of beans to hand from Red kidney beans, to lentils and chickpeas. They don't require soaking and can be very useful to have in any pantry.

Canned Fish Many dishes can use canned or fresh fish. Tuna, crab and anchovies are all useful for salads or pasta dishes.

Pickled Foods Pickles, pickled onions and capers make perfect accompaniments and garnishes for meat and vegetable dishes.

Olives It's always useful to have a can or a bottle of olives. They are delicious in salads, pastas and on pizzas or to blend and make dips from.

Soy Sauce A popular Chinese sauce it is used within all Asian foods and adds a salty flavor. Soy comes in light and dark varieties use the light one with shellfish and the dark one with duck and meat.

Worcestershire Sauce This spicy sauce adds a fantastic fiery flavor to casseroles and soups.

1

Grandma's Breakfast

Eggs Benedict

serves 6

12 very fresh large eggs

12 slices Canadian bacon

6 English muffins

Butter as needed

For the hollandaise

1 cup (2 sticks) unsalted butter

5 large egg yolks

2 tablespoons fresh lemon juice

Cayenne to taste

Salt to taste

To prep the eggs: Working in small batches, poach eggs in a saucepan of very gently simmering salted water to which a tablespoon of white vinegar has been added. As they're done carefully set them into a bowl of cool water. Reserve until needed.

To make the hollandaise: Melt the butter in a small saucepan. Add the egg yolks and lemon juice to a medium bowl. Place over a saucepan with 2 inches of gently simmering water (note: the bowl should not be touching the water). Whisk constantly until the mixture thickens and is very warm to the touch.

Remove from the heat and slowly drizzle in the melted butter, whisking constantly until it's all incorporated. Whisk in the cayenne and salt to taste. Cover with foil and keep in a warm spot until needed.

To complete the plates: Bring a large deep skillet filled with 3 inches of salted water to a simmer. Place the English muffin halves on a baking sheet and toast under the broiler until golden, then brush with butter. Place one slice of Canadian bacon on each muffin half. Turn off the heat and keep the pan in the warm oven until the eggs are reheated.

Carefully transfer the poached eggs into the simmering water for 2 minutes until heated through but still soft. Remove eggs with a slotted spoon, and place one on each muffin half. Spoon over the warm hollandaise and serve immediately.

Spanish Potato Omelet

serves 6

½ cup olive oil
1 pound potatoes, sliced
1 large onion, sliced
1 large garlic clove, crushed
6 large eggs
pinch of salt
Freshly ground black pepper

Heat a nonstick skillet over high heat. Pour in the oil and heat. Reduce the heat, add the potatoes, onion, and garlic and cook for 15–20 minutes, stirring frequently, until the potatoes are tender.

Beat the eggs together in a large bowl and season generously with salt and pepper. Using a slotted spoon, transfer the potatoes and onion to the bowl of eggs. Pour the excess oil left in the skillet into a heatproof pitcher, then scrape off the crusty bits from the base of the skillet.

Reheat the skillet. Add about 2 tablespoons of the oil reserved in the pitcher. Pour in the potato mixture, smoothing the vegetables into an even layer. Cook for about 5 minutes, shaking the skillet occasionally, or until the base of the omelet is set.

Shake the pan and use a spatula to loosen the side of the omelet. Place a large plate face down over the pan. Carefully invert the omelet onto the plate.

Gently slide the omelet back into the skillet, cooked-side up. Use the spatula to "tuck down" the edge. Continue cooking over medium heat for 3–5 minutes until set.

Remove the skillet from the heat and slide the omelet onto a serving plate. Let cool for at least 5 minutes before cutting. Serve hot, warm, or at room temperature.

Banana Cinnamon Muffins

makes 12

¾ cup (1½ sticks) butter

1 cup all-purpose flour

1 teaspoon baking powder

pinch of salt

¾ cup sugar

6 tablespoons milk

2 eggs, lightly beaten

2 small bananas, mashed

Frosting

¼ cup cream cheese

2 tablespoons butter

¼ teaspoon ground cinnamon

1 cup confectioners' sugar

Preheat the oven to 400°F. Lightly grease a 12-cup muffin pan. Sift the flour, baking powder, and salt together into a mixing bowl. Stir in the sugar.

Whisk the milk, eggs, and butter together in a separate bowl until combined. Slowly stir into the flour mixture without beating. Fold in the mashed bananas.

Spoon the mixture into the cups and bake in the preheated oven for 20 minutes until risen and golden. Turn out onto a cooling rack and let cool.

To make the frosting, beat the cream cheese and butter together in a bowl, then beat in the cinnamon and confectioners' sugar until smooth and creamy. Chill the frosting in the refrigerator for about 15 minutes to firm up, then top each muffin with a spoonful.

Potato Pancakes with Smoked Salmon & Dill Sour Cream

serves 8

2¼ pounds Russet potatoes, peeled
½ onion, peeled
2 large eggs
3 tablespoons all-purpose flour
1 teaspoon salt
½ teaspoon freshly ground black pepper
Pinch of cayenne pepper
Vegetable oil, as needed
3 to 4 ounces thinly sliced smoked salmon
4 tablespoons sour cream
¼ cup fresh dill, chopped

Using a cheese grater, shred the potatoes, and quickly transfer into a large bowl of cold water. Grate the onion and add to bowl. Let sit for 20 minutes. Add the eggs, flour, salt, pepper, and cayenne to another large mixing bowl, and whisk until smooth; reserve.

Drain the potato mixture into a colander. Line a baking sheet with several layers of paper towels. Take a handful of the potato mixture from the colander, and squeeze as hard as possible to extract even more water. Place the "dry" potatoes on the paper towels. Spread the potatoes evenly on the baking sheet and press down with some dry paper towels. Remove the paper towels and transfer the potato mixture to the bowl with the egg mixture. Use a spatula to combine thoroughly.

Pour about ¼ inch of vegetable oil into a large, heavy skillet (preferably non-stick). Place over medium-high heat, and when the oil is hot (the surface will begin to shimmer), spoon about ⅓ cup of the potato mixture into the pan, shape into a round, and flatten to about ½ inch thick. Turn down the heat to medium, and fry the potato pancakes for about 5 minutes per side, or until browned and crispy.

Remember, the potatoes are raw, so be sure they cook through. There is nothing worse than raw potatoes! You can probably fry 4 potato pancakes at a time. Drain on paper towels and hold in a warm oven until they're all done.

To serve, top with the sliced smoked salmon, a dollop of sour cream, the fresh dill, and a few grinds of black pepper.

Corned Beef Hash

serves 6

2 tablespoons butter

1 tablespoon vegetable oil

1½ pounds cooked corned beef, cut in small cubes

1 medium onion, diced

1½ pounds white potatoes, peeled, cut in small cubes

Salt and fresh ground black pepper to taste

¼ teaspoon paprika

¼ teaspoon garlic powder

¼ cup diced green bell pepper, or jalapeño if a spicier version is desired

2 tablespoons prepared roasted tomato salsa

1 tablespoon freshly sliced chives

Add the butter, oil, corned beef, and onions to a large, cold, non-stick or well-seasoned cast iron skillet. Turn heat to medium-low and cook, stirring occasionally, while you prepare the potatoes.

In a saucepan, boil the potatoes in salted water for about 5 to 7 minutes (depending on the size), until partially cooked, but still very firm. Drain very well and add to the skillet along with the rest of the ingredients.

Mix together thoroughly with the hot corned beef mixture, and press down slightly with a spatula to flatten. Turn up the heat to medium. Every 10 minutes or so, turn the mixture over with a spatula to bring the crusty bottom, up to the top. Do this several times until the mixture is well-browned. Take your time – the only real secret to great corned beef hash is to make sure it cooks long enough, so the potatoes are crisp-edged, and the cubes of meat get nicely caramelized.

Taste for salt and pepper, and adjust if necessary. Transfer to plates, and top with poached eggs. Garnish with freshly chopped chives.

New Orleans Style French Toast

serves 1-6

5 large eggs
1 cup milk
½ cup cream
Pinch of salt
1 tablespoon sugar
2 teaspoons vanilla
½ teaspoon cinnamon
Pinch allspice
12 thick slices day-old French bread (use a regular sized loaf, not the skinny baguette type)
6 tablespoons butter, plus more as needed

Pre-heat oven to 375°F.

In a large mixing bowl, whisk together the eggs, milk, cream, salt, sugar, vanilla, cinnamon, and allspice. Soak the bread slices in the custard mixture for at least 20 minutes, or until completely saturated.

In a large non-stick skillet, lightly brown the slices in batches, in a few tablespoons of butter over medium heat; about 2 minutes per side. Don't cook too dark, as additional browning will occur in the oven.

Transfer to lightly buttered, foil-lined sheet pans, and bake for 10 minutes. After 10 minutes, remove, and turn each slice over. Put back in the oven for another 10 to 15 minutes, or until browned and the bread springs back slightly when tested with a finger.

Serve immediately.

Lemon Poppy Seed Muffins

makes 16

2 cups all-purpose flour
½ teaspoon salt
1½ teaspoons baking powder
¼ teaspoon baking soda
½ cup (1 stick) unsalted butter, softened
1 cup sugar
Finely grated zest from 2 lemons
2 large eggs
2 tablespoons lemon juice
1 cup sour cream
2 tablespoons poppy seeds

For the glaze
1 tablespoon lemon juice
3 tablespoons confectioners' sugar

Preheat oven to 350°F. Whisk together the flour, salt, baking powder, and baking soda in a bowl, and reserve until needed.

In a mixing bowl, beat the butter, sugar, and lemon zest, until light and creamy. Beat in the eggs one at a time, mixing thoroughly before adding the next. Stir in a third of the flour mixture until just combined. Stir in the lemon juice, and half of the sour cream until combined.

Add half of the remaining flour mixture, and stir until combined. Stir in the remaining sour cream. Stir in the rest of the flour mixture, and then the poppy seeds.

Line a 12-cup muffin tin with paper baking cups. Fill each to the top with batter. Bake about 30 minutes, or until golden brown and a tester inserted in the center comes out clean. While the muffins are baking, mix the lemon juice and confectioners' sugar together to form a thin glaze.

Remove the muffins from the oven when ready, and allow to cool for 5 minutes. Brush the lemon glaze evenly over the top of each muffin. This is not intended to be a frosting, but just a very light glaze to give the tops a little shine and extra kiss of lemon flavor. When cool enough to handle, remove muffins from the tins and cool completely on a rack before serving.

Baked Spinach & Feta Omelet

serves 6

1 pound fresh spinach leaves, washed

1 tablespoon butter

6 slices bacon, cut in ¼ inch pieces

½ onion, diced

12 eggs, beaten

Salt and freshly ground black pepper to taste

Pinch of cayenne

1 cup feta cheese, crumbled

Pre-heat oven to 350°F.

Put a large stockpot over high heat. Add the butter, and as soon as it melts, dump in all the spinach and cover the pot quickly. Leave for one minute, uncover, and continue cooking, stirring the spinach with a long wooden spoon, until just wilted. Transfer to a colander to drain. When the spinach is cool enough to handle, squeeze as much liquid out as possible, and roughly chop. Reserve until needed.

In a 10 to 12 inch ovenproof skillet, cook the bacon over medium heat until almost crisp, add the onions and a pinch of salt, and continue cooking until the onions are translucent, about 6 to 7 minutes. Any excess bacon fat can be removed at this point.

Stir in the spinach. Season with salt, freshly ground black pepper, and cayenne to taste. When the spinach is heated through, add the eggs and stir with a spatula to combine thoroughly. Turn off the heat, and top with the crumbled feta cheese. Use the spatula to press the cheese down into the egg slightly.

Bake for 10 minutes, then finish under the broiler for about 3 minutes, or until the eggs are just set, and the top is lightly browned. Let rest for 5 to 10 minutes before slicing and serving.

Mexican Eggs

serves 4

8 large eggs
2 tablespoons milk
pepper
1 teaspoon olive oil
1 red bell pepper, seeded and thinly sliced
½ fresh red chile
1 fresh chorizo sausage, skinned and sliced
4 tablespoons chopped fresh cilantro
4 slices toasted whole wheat bread, for serving

Beat the eggs, milk, and pepper to taste in a large bowl. Set aside.

Heat the oil in a nonstick skillet over medium heat, add the bell pepper and chile and cook, stirring frequently, for 5 minutes, or until the bell pepper is soft and browned in places. Add the chorizo and cook until just browned. Transfer to a warmed plate and set aside.

Return the skillet to the heat, add the egg mixture, and cook to a soft scramble. Add the chorizo mixture, stir to combine, and sprinkle over the cilantro.

Serve at once on the toasted bread.

Chocolate Chip Muffins

makes 12

3 tablespoons soft butter, plus extra for greasing
1 cup sugar
2 large eggs
⅔ cup plain yogurt
5 tablespoons milk
2 cups all-purpose flour
1 teaspoon baking soda
1 cup semisweet chocolate chips

Preheat the oven to 400°F. Lightly grease a 12-cup muffin pan.

Place the butter and sugar in a mixing bowl and beat with a wooden spoon until light and fluffy. Beat in the eggs, yogurt, and milk until combined.

Sift the flour and baking soda into the batter. Stir until just blended.

Stir in the chocolate chips, then divide the batter evenly among the cups and bake in the oven for 25 minutes, or until risen and golden.

Remove the muffins from the oven and let cool in the pan for 5 minutes, then place them on a cooling rack to cool completely.

Sausage and Mushroom Breakfast Fritata

serves 6-8

2 tablespoons butter

1½ pounds potatoes, peeled, cut into 1 inch chunks

1 pound sweet or hot Italian sausage (or sausage of your choice), casing removed

1 bunch green onions, chopped

1½ cups shredded cheddar cheese, divided

3 cups sliced button mushrooms

14 eggs, beaten

¼ cup milk

1½ teaspoon salt

½ teaspoon fresh ground black pepper

Dash of Tabasco, optional

Pre-heat oven to 300°F.

Boil the potatoes in salted water until just tender, and drain well. Grease a 13 x 9 inch baking dish with 1 tablespoon of the butter, and add the potatoes. Top with half the cheese.

Brown the sausage in a skillet over medium heat, breaking it into small pieces with a spatula or wooden spoon as it cooks. When browned, add the green onions and cook for 2 minutes more. Use a slotted spoon to transfer the sausage and onions into the baking dish.

Pour off any excess grease from the pan, and add the butter and mushrooms. Add a pinch of salt and cook, stirring, over high heat until well-browned. Add mushrooms to the baking dish and distribute evenly.

Whisk together the eggs, milk, salt, freshly ground black pepper, and Tabasco in a mixing bowl. Pour over the sausage and mushrooms. Give the baking dish a jiggle or two, to make sure the eggs are distributed. Top with the rest of the cheese.

Bake for about 35 minutes, or until just set. If desired, place under a hot broiler for a minute or two to brown the top. Let rest at least 15 minutes before serving.

Buttermilk Biscuits

makes 12-14

2 cups all-purpose flour

2 teaspoons baking powder

¼ teaspoon baking soda

1 teaspoon salt

7 tablespoons unsalted butter, cut into thin slices, chilled in freezer

¾ cup cold buttermilk

Pre-heat oven to 425°F.

In a mixing bowl, whisk together the dry ingredients to thoroughly combine. Cut in the ice cold butter slices using a wire pastry blender, until the mixture has the texture of coarse crumbs.

Make a well in the center and pour in the cold buttermilk. Stir the dry ingredients into the buttermilk with a fork until a loose, sticky dough is formed. Stop as soon as the mixture comes together. Form into a ball and turn the dough out onto a floured work surface.

With floured hands, pat the dough into a rectangle (about 8 x 4 inch-thick). Fold dough in thirds (like folding a letter-sized piece of paper). Repeat this process twice more.

On a lightly-floured surface, roll or pat the dough out about ½ inch thick. Cut with a round biscuit cutter, and place on a parchment or silicon mat-lined baking sheet, a few inches apart. You can gather up any extra dough after cutting, and repeat to get a few more biscuits, although the texture may suffer from the extra working.

Make a slight depression in the center of each biscuit with your thumb (to help them rise evenly). Brush the tops lightly with buttermilk. Bake for about 15 minutes, or until risen and golden brown. Cool on a rack for 10 minutes before serving.

Cinnamon Swirl French Toast

serves 6

1 package store-bought cinnamon buns (6)
4 eggs
1 cup whole milk
1 teaspoon vanilla extract
1 tablespoon sugar
Pinch of salt
1 teaspoon ground cinnamon
2 tablespoons butter
Butter and maple syrup for serving.

Slice the Cinnamon Swirl Buns in half horizontally.

Combine the eggs, milk, sugar, vanilla, and salt in a large, shallow bowl.

Layer the cinnamon bun slices into the mixture, flipping to coat both sides thoroughly.

Melt the butter in a large frying pan over a medium heat. In batches, fry the cinnamon bun slices until golden and cooked through. Cook both sides. Allow 3-4 minutes per side.

Blueberry Pancakes

makes 10-12

1 cup all-purpose flour
2 tablespoons white sugar
2 teaspoons baking powder
½ teaspoon salt
1 cup buttermilk
3 tablespoons butter, melted
1 large egg
1 cup blueberries, rinsed and patted dry

To serve
Butter
Warm maple syrup

Pre-heat oven to 275°F.

Sift the flour, sugar, baking powder, and salt together into a large bowl and make a well in the center.

Beat the buttermilk, butter, and egg together in a separate small bowl, then pour the mixture into the well in the dry ingredients. Beat the dry ingredients into the liquid, gradually drawing them in from the side, until a smooth batter forms. Gently stir in the blueberries.

Heat a large skillet over medium-high heat until a splash of water dances on the surface. Use a pastry brush or crumpled piece of paper towel and the oil to lightly grease the base of the skillet.

Use a ladle to drop about 4 tablespoons of batter into the skillet and spread it out into a 4 inch round. Continue adding as many pancakes as will fit in your skillet. Leave the pancakes to cook until small bubbles appear on the surface, then flip them over and cook for a further 1 to 2 minutes until the bottoms are golden brown.

Transfer the pancakes to a warmed plate and keep warm in the oven while you cook the remaining batter, lightly greasing the skillet as before. Serve with a pat of butter on top of each pancake and warm maple syrup for pouring over.

2

Grandma's Soup & Snacks

Corn and Clam Chowder

serves 4

1 pound 10 ounces fresh clams

2 tablespoons dry white wine

½ stick (¼ cup) butter

1 large onion, finely chopped

1 small carrot, finely diced

3 tablespoons all-purpose flour

1¼ cups fish stock

¾ cup water (if using canned clams)

1 pound (3 medium) potatoes, diced

1 cup corn, thawed if frozen

2 cups whole milk

Salt and pepper

Chopped fresh parsley, to garnish

If using fresh clams, wash under cold running water. Discard any with broken shells or any that refuse to close when tapped. Put the clams into a heavy-bottom saucepan with the wine. Cover tightly, set over medium-high heat, and cook for 2 to 4 minutes, or until they open, shaking the pan occasionally. Discard any that remain closed. Remove the clams from the shells and strain the cooking liquid through a very fine mesh sieve; reserve both.

Melt the butter in a large saucepan over medium-low heat. Add the onion and carrot and cook for 3 to 4 minutes, stirring frequently, until the onion is softened. Stir in the flour and continue cooking for 2 minutes.

Slowly add about half the stock and stir well, scraping the bottom of the pan to mix in the flour. Pour in the remaining stock and the reserved clam cooking liquid, and bring just to a boil, stirring.

Add the potatoes, corn, and milk and stir to combine. Reduce the heat and simmer gently, partially covered, for about 20 minutes, stirring occasionally, until all the vegetables are tender.

Chop the clams, if large. Stir in the clams and continue cooking for about 5 minutes until heated through. Taste and adjust the seasoning, if needed. Ladle the soup into bowls and sprinkle with parsley.

Deviled Eggs

makes 24

12 large eggs
1 teaspoon white wine vinegar
4 tablespoons mayonnaise
½ teaspoon Dijon mustard
½ teaspoon prepared horseradish
¼ teaspoon Worcestershire sauce
½ teaspoon salt
Dash of Tabasco
Pinch of cayenne pepper
Paprika or more cayenne pepper to garnish
1 tablespoon thinly sliced chives

Place the eggs in a single layer in a large saucepan and cover with cold water by one inch. Bring the water to a boil over high heat. Turn off the heat, and cover tightly with the lid, and set a timer for 17 minutes.

Carefully pour off most the hot water, and fill the pan with cold water. Allow to sit for 3 minutes. Pour off most of the water, and again fill the pan with cold water. Leave for 15 minutes. Drain and refrigerate the eggs until needed.

Peel the eggs under cold running water. Cut the eggs in half lengthwise and pop out the yolks into a small mixing bowl. Add the vinegar, mayonnaise, mustard, horseradish, Worcestershire, salt, Tabasco, and cayenne. Mash and mix with a wire whisk until smooth and light.

Using a spoon, or pastry bag with a star tip, fill the egg white halves with the yolk mixture. Sprinkle tops with paprika or cayenne pepper. Chill before serving with the sliced chives.

Hot Spinach and Artichoke Dip

serves 8

- 2 tablespoons butter
- ½ cup chopped scallions, white and light green parts only
- Pinch of salt
- 2 cloves garlic, finely minced
- 1 package (10 ounces) frozen chopped spinach, thawed, drained, squeezed dry
- One (14.5 ounce) can artichoke hearts, drained, roughly chopped
- 1 cup cream cheese
- ¼ cup sour cream
- ¼ teaspoon hot sauce
- Small pinch of nutmeg
- ½ cup grated Parmesan cheese, preferably Parmigiano Reggiano
- ½ cup grated mozzarella cheese

Preheat oven to 400°F. Sauté the onions with a pinch of salt in the butter over medium heat until translucent. Add the garlic, stir to combine, and immediately turn off the heat; reserve.

In a mixing bowl, combine the spinach, artichoke hearts, cream cheese, sour cream, hot sauce, nutmeg, and Parmesan cheese. Add the onion mixture, and stir until thoroughly mixed.

Transfer the mixture into a small baking dish, and top with the mozzarella cheese. Bake until bubbling and golden, about 25 minutes. The dip may be placed under a hot broiler for a few minutes, if a browner top is desired.

Deep-fried Chili Corn Balls

serves 4

6 scallions, sliced
3 tablespoons chopped fresh cilantro
1 cup canned corn
1 teaspoon mild chili powder
1 tablespoon sweet chili sauce
¼ cup shredded coconut
1 egg
⅓ cup cornmeal
Oil, for deep-frying
Extra sweet chili sauce, for serving

In a large bowl, mix together the scallions, cilantro, corn, chili powder, chili sauce, coconut, egg, and cornmeal until well blended.

Cover the bowl with plastic wrap and let stand for about 10 minutes.

Heat the oil for deep-frying in a large preheated wok or skillet to 350°F or until a cube of bread browns in 30 seconds.

Carefully drop spoonfuls of the chili and cornmeal mixture into the hot oil. Deep-fry the chili corn balls, in batches, for 4–5 minutes or until crispy and a deep golden brown color.

Remove the chili corn balls with a slotted spoon, transfer to paper towels, and let drain thoroughly.

Transfer the chili corn balls to serving plates and serve with extra sweet chili sauce, for dipping.

Baked Herb Ricotta

serves 4

1 tablespoon olive oil, plus extra for drizzling

2 pounds 4 ounces ricotta cheese, drained

3 eggs, lightly beaten

3 tablespoons chopped fresh herbs, such as tarragon, parsley, dill, and chives

½ teaspoon paprika, plus extra for sprinkling

4 slices whole wheat bread

Pepper

Salad greens, for serving

Preheat the oven to 350°F.

Grease a 9 x 5 x 3-inch loaf pan and line with parchment paper.

Put the ricotta into a bowl and beat well. Add the eggs and stir until smooth, then stir in the fresh herbs, pepper and paprika.

Spoon the mixture into the prepared pan and put into a roasting pan half-filled with water.

Bake in the preheated oven for 30–40 minutes, or until set. Remove from the oven and let cool.

Meanwhile, cut the crusts off the bread and toast on both sides. Cut through each slice widthwise and cut each slice diagonally into triangles. Arrange in a single layer on a baking sheet and bake in the oven for 10 minutes.

Turn out the baked ricotta onto a serving dish, drizzle with a little oil, and sprinkle with paprika. Serve with the toast and salad greens.

Buffalo Chicken Wings

makes 40

4 pounds chicken wings

1 tablespoon vegetable oil

1 tablespoon all-purpose flour

1 teaspoon salt

For the sauce

2/3 cup hot sauce

½ cup (1 stick) cold unsalted butter, cut into 1-inch slices

1½ tablespoons white vinegar

¼ teaspoon Worcestershire sauce

1 teaspoon Tabasco

¼ teaspoon cayenne pepper

Pinch of garlic powder

Salt

Preheat oven to 425°F. If the chicken wings being used were frozen and thawed, be sure they're completely dry before starting recipe. If using whole wings, cut each into two pieces (in wing-speak called the "flat" and the "drum"). The small wing tips can be discarded, or saved for stock. In a large mixing bowl, toss the wings with the oil, flour, and salt until evenly coated.

Line two heavy-duty baking sheets with lightly greased foil or silicon baking mats. Divide the wings and spread out evenly. Do not crowd. Bake for 25 minutes, remove, and turn the wings over. Return to the oven and cook another 20 to 30 minutes, or until the wings are well-browned and cooked through.

Note: Cooking times will vary based on size of the wings. When fully cooked, the bones will easily pull out from the meat.

While the wings are baking, mix all the sauce ingredients in a saucepan. Bring to a simmer, whisking, over medium heat. Remove from heat and reserve. Taste sauce; adjust for salt and spiciness, if desired.

After the wings are cooked, transfer to a large mixing bowl. Pour the warm sauce over the hot wings and toss with a spoon or spatula to completely coat.

Beef Soup with Rice

serves 4

- **12 ounces lean beef**
- **4 cups beef stock**
- **1 cinnamon stick, broken in 2**
- **2 tablespoons dark soy sauce**
- **2 tablespoons dry sherry**
- **3 tablespoons tomato paste**
- **One 8-ounce can water chestnuts, drained and sliced**
- **1 cup cooked white rice**
- **1 teaspoon finely grated orange rind**
- **6 tablespoons orange juice**
- **Pinch of salt**
- **Freshly ground black pepper**
- **Strips of orange rind**
- **2 tablespoons chopped fresh chives, for garnish**

Carefully trim away any fat from the beef. Cut the beef into thin strips and then place in a large pan.

Pour in the stock and add the cinnamon, soy sauce, sherry, tomato paste, and water chestnuts. Bring to a boil over medium heat, skimming off any foam that rises to the surface with a flat ladle or skimmer. Cover the pan, reduce the heat, and simmer gently for about 20 minutes or until the beef strips are tender.

Skim the soup again to remove any more foam. Remove and discard the cinnamon stick and blot the surface of the soup with absorbent paper towels to remove as much fat as possible.

Stir in the rice, grated orange rind, and orange juice. Season with salt and pepper to taste. Heat through for 2–3 minutes before ladling into warmed bowls.

Serve garnished with the strips of orange rind and chopped chives.

Stuffed Tomatoes

serves 4

4 large tomatoes

2 tablespoons finely chopped fresh basil

4 teaspoons olive oil

2 cups white mushrooms, very finely chopped

1 small onion, very finely chopped

2 garlic cloves, very finely chopped

1 tablespoon chopped fresh parsley

1 cup vegetable stock

1 tablespoon freshly grated Parmesan cheese

Salt and pepper

Sprigs of fresh basil, for garnish

Preheat the oven to 350°F.

Slice a lid from the top of each tomato and reserve. Using a teaspoon, carefully scoop out the flesh from the tomato shells and chop. Place it in a bowl and add 1 teaspoon of the basil. Invert the tomato shells on paper towels to drain.

Heat 1 tablespoon of the oil in a skillet. Add the mushrooms, onion, garlic, parsley, and the remaining basil and season with pepper to taste. Cover and cook over low heat for 2 minutes, then remove the lid and cook, stirring occasionally, for an additional 8–10 minutes.

Meanwhile, bring the stock to a boil in a pan and cook until reduced by about three-quarters. Stir in the chopped tomato mixture and cook for an additional 3–4 minutes until thickened. Push the mixture through a strainer with a wooden spoon and stir it into the mushroom mixture. Stir in the Parmesan cheese.

Stand the tomatoes in an ovenproof dish and season the insides with salt. Fill each tomato with stuffing and replace the lids. Brush with the remaining oil and bake for about 15 minutes, or until tender and cooked through. Serve warm.

Maryland Crab Cakes with Tartar Sauce

makes 6

1 large egg, beaten

2 tablespoons mayonnaise

½ teaspoon Dijon mustard

¼ teaspoon Worcestershire sauce

½ teaspoon Old Bay seasoning

¼ teaspoon salt

Pinch of cayenne pepper

1 pound fresh lump crabmeat, well drained

10 saltine crackers

Plain breadcrumbs

1 tablespoon vegetable oil

2 tablespoons unsalted butter

For the tartar sauce

1 cup mayonnaise

¼ cup sweet pickle relish

1 tablespoon finely minced onion

1 tablespoon chopped capers

1 tablespoon chopped parsley

1½ tablespoons freshly squeezed lemon juice

Dash of Worcestershire sauce

Few drops of Tabasco

Salt and pepper

Whisk together the egg, mayonnaise, mustard, Worcestershire, Old Bay, salt, and cayenne to a mixing bowl. Crush the crackers into very fine crumbs and add to the bowl. Stir until combined. Let sit for 5 minutes.

Gently fold in the crabmeat. Cover the bowl and refrigerate for at least 1 hour.

Sprinkle the breadcrumbs lightly over a large plate. Shape the crab mixture into 6 cakes, and place on the plate. Dust the tops of each crab cake lightly with more breadcrumbs. These cakes are almost all crab, which makes them fragile. They will bind together as the egg cooks, and golden-brown crust forms.

Heat the vegetable oil and butter in a large skillet over medium-high heat. When the foam from the butter begins to dissipate, carefully transfer each crab cake to the pan. Sauté until golden brown, about 4 minutes per side. Drain on a paper towel, and serve with the sauce.

For the sauce: Mix together all the ingredients in a bowl. Refrigerate at least an hour before serving. Makes 1½ cups.

Potato & Spinach Triangles

serves 4

2 tablespoons butter, melted, plus extra for greasing
1½ cups finely diced waxy potatoes
1 pound frozen spinach, thawed
1 tomato, seeded and chopped
¼ teaspoon chili powder
½ teaspoon lemon juice
One 8-ounce pack filo pastry, thawed, if frozen
Pinch of salt
Freshly ground black pepper

Lemon mayonnaise
⅔ cup mayonnaise
2 teaspoons lemon juice
Zest of 1 lemon

Preheat the oven to 375F

Lightly grease a baking sheet.

Bring a pan of lightly salted water to a boil and cook the potatoes for 10 minutes, or until cooked through. Drain thoroughly and place in a mixing bowl.

Drain the spinach thoroughly, squeezing out excess moisture, and add to the potato. Stir in the tomato, chili powder, and lemon juice. Season with salt and pepper.

Lightly brush 8 sheets of filo pastry with melted butter. Spread out 4 of the sheets and lay the other 4 on top of each. Cut them into rectangles about 8 x 4 inches.

Spoon the potato and spinach mixture onto one end of each rectangle. Fold a corner of the pastry over the filling, fold the pointed end back over the pastry strip, then fold over the remaining pastry to form a triangle.

Place the triangles on the baking sheet and bake for 20 minutes, or until golden brown.

To make the lemon mayonnaise, mix the mayonnaise, lemon juice, and lemon zest together in a small bowl. Serve the potato and spinach triangles warm or cold with the lemon mayonnaise.

Refried Beans with Tortillas

serves 4

2 tablespoons olive oil
1 onion, finely chopped
3 garlic cloves, finely chopped
1 green chile, chopped
One 15-ounce can red kidney beans, drained
One 15-ounce can pinto beans, drained
2 tablespoons chopped fresh cilantro
2/3 cup vegetable stock
8 wheat tortillas
1/2 cup cheddar cheese, grated
Salt and pepper

Relish

4 scallions, chopped
1 red onion, chopped
1 green chile, chopped
1 tablespoon garlic-flavored wine vinegar
1 teaspoon sugar
1 tomato, chopped

Preheat oven to 350°F.

Heat the oil in a large skillet. Add the onion and sauté for 3–5 minutes. Add the garlic and chile and cook for 1 minute.

Mash the beans with a potato masher and stir into the pan with the cilantro.

Stir in the stock and cook the beans, stirring, for 5 minutes until soft and pulpy.

Place the tortillas on a baking sheet and heat through in a warm oven for 1–2 minutes.

Mix together the relish ingredients.

Spoon the beans into a serving dish and top with the cheese. Season well. Roll the tortillas and serve with the relish and beans.

Shrimp Fritters

serves 4

12 ounces potatoes
3 sticks celery, chopped
1 carrot
½ small onion
12 ounces shelled cooked shrimp, thawed, if frozen
2½ tablespoons all-purpose flour
1 egg, lightly beaten
Vegetable oil, for frying
Salt and pepper

Cherry tomato salsa

12 cherry tomatoes, cut into quarters
½ small mango, finely diced
1 fresh red chile, seeded and finely chopped
½ small red onion, finely chopped
1 tablespoon chopped fresh cilantro
1 tablespoon chopped fresh chives
2 tablespoons olive oil
2 teaspoons lemon juice
Salt and pepper

For the salsa, mix the tomatoes, mango, chile, onion, cilantro, chives, olive oil, lemon juice, and seasoning. Set aside for the flavors to steep.

Using a food processor or the fine blade of a box grater, finely grate the potatoes, celery root, carrot, and onion. Combine with the shrimp, flour, and egg. Season well and set aside.

Divide the shrimp mixture into 8 equal pieces. Press each into a greased 4 inch metal pastry cutter (if you have only 1 cutter, you can simply shape the fritters individually).

Heat a shallow layer of oil in a large skillet. When hot, transfer the fritters, still in the cutters, to the skillet, in 4 batches if necessary. When the oil sizzles underneath, remove the cutter.

Cook gently, pressing down with a spatula, for 6–8 minutes on each side, until crisp and browned and the vegetables are tender. Drain on paper towels and keep warm while you cook the remainder. Serve hot with the tomato salsa.

Roasted Onion & Pepper Tartlets

serves 4

1 pack (9-ounces) puff pastry, thawed, if frozen

2 medium red onions

1 red bell pepper

8 cherry tomatoes, halved

1 cup shredded mozzarella cheese

6-8 sprigs of fresh thyme

Preheat the broiler.

Roll out the pastry to make four 3-inch squares. Using a sharp knife, trim the edges of the pastry and reserve the trimmings. Place the pastry squares on a baking sheet. Brush a little water along each edge of the pastry squares and use the reserved pastry trimmings to make a rim around each tartlet. Chill the pastry in the refrigerator for 30 minutes.

While the pastry is chilling, prepare the vegetables. Cut the red onions into thin wedges; halve and seed the bell pepper. Place the onions and bell pepper in a shallow roasting pan. Cook under the preheated broiler for 15 minutes or until the pepper is charred. Place the roasted bell pepper halves in a plastic bag and let sweat for 10 minutes. Peel off the skin from the bell peppers and cut the flesh into strips.

Reduce the oven temperature to 400°F. Remove the pastry from the refrigerator, and line the pastry squares with squares of foil. Bake for 10 minutes. Remove the foil.

Arrange the roasted onions, bell pepper strips, tomatoes, and cheese evenly among the four tartlets, and sprinkle each with fresh thyme. Return the tartlets to the oven and bake for 15 minutes or until the pastry is golden. Serve hot.

Bacon & Lentil Soup

serves 4

1 pound thick, rindless smoked bacon strips, diced
1 onion, chopped
2 carrots, sliced
2 celery stalks, chopped
1 turnip, chopped
1 large potato, chopped
½ cup green lentils
4 cups chicken stock or water
Salt and pepper
1 tablespoon dried mixed herbs

Heat a large, heavy pan. Add the bacon and cook over low heat, stirring frequently, for 4–5 minutes, until the fat runs. Add the onion, carrots, celery, turnip, and potato and cook, stirring frequently, for 5 minutes.

Add the lentils and mixed herbs and pour in the stock. Bring to a boil, then transfer the mixture to the slow cooker. Cover and cook on low for 8–9 hours, or until the lentils are tender.

Season the soup to taste with pepper and salt, if necessary. Ladle into warmed soup bowls and serve.

Chicken & Corn Soup

serves 4

1 large, 6 ounce skinless boneless chicken breast
2 tablespoons vegetable oil
3 scallions, thinly sliced diagonally
½ large red bell pepper, thinly sliced
1 garlic clove, crushed
one 7-ounce can whole baby corn, thinly sliced
4 cups chicken stock
One 11 ounce can corn, well drained
2 tablespoons sherry
3 teaspoons sweet chili sauce
3 teaspoons cornstarch
2 tomatoes, cut into quarters, seeded, and sliced
Pinch salt
Freshly ground black pepper

Cut the chicken breast into 4 strips lengthwise, then cut each strip into narrow slices across the grain.

Heat the oil in a wok or skillet, swirling it around until it is really hot.

Add the chicken and stir-fry for 3–4 minutes, moving it around the wok until it is well sealed all over and almost cooked through.

Add the scallions, bell pepper, and garlic, and stir-fry for 2–3 minutes. Add the sliced baby corn and stock and bring to a boil.

Add the corn, sherry, sweet chili sauce, and salt to taste, and simmer for 5 minutes, stirring from time to time.

Blend the cornstarch with a little cold water. Add to the soup and bring to a boil, stirring until the sauce is thickened. Add the tomato slices, season to taste, and simmer for 1–2 minutes.

Serve hot, sprinkled with the cilantro or parsley

Fresh Tomato Tartlets

serves 6

One package (9 ounces) ready-made puff pie dough, thawed, if frozen

1 egg, beaten

2 tablespoons pesto

6 plum tomatoes, sliced

Salt and pepper

Fresh thyme leaves, for garnish (optional)

Preheat oven to 400°F.

On a lightly floured counter, roll out the pie dough to a rectangle measuring 12 x 10 inches.

Cut the rectangle in half and divide each half into 3 pieces to make 6 even-size rectangles. Chill in the refrigerator for 20 minutes.

Lightly score the edges of the pie dough rectangles and brush with the beaten egg.

Spread the pesto over the rectangles, dividing it equally among them, leaving a 1-inch border around each one.

Arrange the tomato slices along the center of each rectangle on top of the pesto.

Season well with salt and pepper to taste and lightly sprinkle with fresh thyme leaves, if using.

Bake the tarts for 15–20 minutes, until well risen and golden brown.

Transfer the tomato tartlets to warmed serving plates straight from the oven and serve while they are still piping hot and crisp.

Minestrone Soup

serves 4

2 tablespoons olive oil
2 garlic cloves, chopped
2 red onions, chopped
4 ounces prosciutto, sliced
1 red bell pepper, seeded and chopped
1 orange bell pepper, seeded and chopped
One 14.5 ounce can chopped tomatoes
4 cups vegetable stock
1 celery stalk, trimmed and sliced
One 10.5 ounce can borlotti beans, drained
½ small green leafy cabbage, shredded
¾ cup frozen peas, thawed
1 tablespoon chopped fresh parsley
Salt and pepper
4 ounces dried vermicelli
Freshly grated Parmesan cheese, to garnish
Fresh crusty bread, to serve

Heat the oil in a large pan. Add the garlic, onions, and prosciutto and cook over medium heat, stirring, for 3 minutes, until slightly softened.

Add the red and orange bell peppers and the chopped tomatoes and cook for another 2 minutes, stirring.

Stir in the stock, then add the celery, beans, cabbage, peas, and parsley. Season with salt and pepper. Bring to a boil, then lower the heat and simmer for 30 minutes.

Add the vermicelli to the pan. Cook for another 10–12 minutes, or according to the instructions on the package.

Remove from the heat and ladle into serving bowls. Garnish with freshly grated Parmesan and serve with fresh crusty bread.

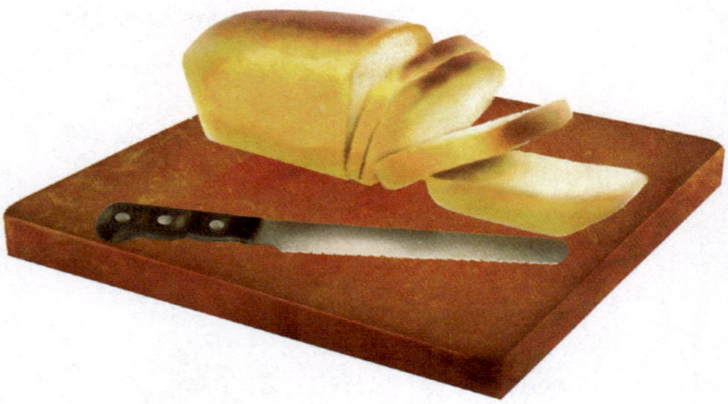

Warm Crab Dip

serves 8–11

- **1¾ cups cream cheese**
- **¾ cup cheddar cheese, grated**
- **1 cup sour cream**
- **4 tablespoons mayonnaise**
- **2 tablespoons lemon juice**
- **2 teaspoons Dijon mustard**
- **2 teaspoons Worcestershire sauce, plus extra to taste**
- **1 lb 2 ounces cooked fresh crabmeat**
- **1 garlic clove, halved**
- **Salt and pepper**
- **Butter, for greasing**
- **Sprigs of fresh dill, for garnish**
- **Savory crackers, for serving**

Put the cream cheese into a bowl and stir in the cheese, sour cream, mayonnaise, lemon juice, mustard, and Worcestershire sauce.

Add the crabmeat and salt and pepper to taste and gently stir together. Taste and add extra Worcestershire sauce, if desired. Cover and let chill for 24 hours.

When you are ready to heat the dip, remove it from the refrigerator and let it come to room temperature.

Meanwhile, preheat the oven to 350°F. Rub the cut sides of the garlic clove over the base and sides of an ovenproof dish suitable for serving from, then lightly grease.

Spoon the crab mixture into the dish and smooth the surface. Heat the dip through in the oven for 15 minutes.

Crispy Chicken Fingers with Honey Mustard Dip

serves 8

1 cup all-purpose flour
2 teaspoons salt
1 teaspoon garlic salt
1 teaspoon chipotle pepper
½ teaspoon white pepper
4 large skinless, boneless chicken breasts, cut into ½-inch strips
4 eggs, beaten
1 tablespoon milk
3 cups Japanese-style panko bread crumbs
Vegetable oil for frying

For the dip

½ cup mayonnaise
2 tablespoons Dijon mustard
2 tablespoons yellow mustard
1 tablespoon rice vinegar
2 tablespoons honey
½ teaspoon hot sauce, optional

Combine the flour, salt, garlic salt, chipotle, and white pepper in a large, sealable plastic freezer bag. Shake to mix. Add the chicken strips, seal the bag, and shake vigorously to coat evenly.

In a mixing bowl, whisk together the eggs and milk. Add the chicken strips, shaking off the excess flour as you remove them from the bag. Stir until the strips are completely coated in the egg mixture.

Pour the breadcrumbs in a shallow pan. Use one hand (called the "wet" hand) to remove the chicken strips from the bowl of eggs, a few at a time, allowing the excess egg to drip off, and place in the pan of panko. Use the other hand (called the "dry" hand) to coat the chicken in the breadcrumbs, pressing them in firmly. As they are breaded, place the strips on baking sheets or racks. When done breading, let the chicken strips rest for 10 to 15 minutes before frying.

Pour about ½ inch of oil in a large, heavy skillet (ideally cast iron) and set over medium-high heat. When the oil is hot enough to fry (350°F to 375°F or test with a small piece of breading), cook for 2 to 3 minutes per side, or until golden brown and cooked through. Work in batches; drain on paper towels or baking racks, and keep the cooked chicken fingers in a warm oven (175°F) until all are done.

To make the honey mustard dip: Combine all the ingredients and mix well. Serve immediately.

Tuna-stuffed Tomatoes

serves 4

4 large tomatoes
2 tablespoons dried tomato paste
2 egg yolks
2 teaspoons lemon juice
Finely grated rind of 1 lemon
4 tablespoons olive oil
One 5 ounce can tuna, drained of oil
2 tablespoons capers, rinsed
Pinch of salt
Freshly ground black pepper
2 sun-dried tomatoes, cut into strips
Fresh basil leaves, for garnish

Preheat the oven to 400°F.

Halve the tomatoes and scoop out the seeds. Divide the sun-dried tomato paste among the tomato halves and spread around the inside of the skin.

Place on a baking sheet and roast in the oven for 12–15 minutes. Let cool slightly.

Meanwhile, in a food processor, blend the egg yolks and lemon juice with the lemon rind until smooth. Once mixed, and with the motor still running slowly, add the olive oil. Stop the processor as soon as the mayonnaise has thickened. Alternatively, use a hand whisk, beating the mixture continuously until it thickens.

Add the tuna and capers to the mayonnaise and season.

Spoon the tuna mayonnaise mixture into the tomato shells and garnish with the sun-dried tomato strips and basil leaves. Return the stuffed tomatoes to the oven for a few minutes or serve chilled.

Vegetable Soup with Cannellini Beans

serves 4

1 small eggplant
2 large tomatoes
1 potato, peeled
1 carrot, peeled
1 leek
One 14.5 ounce can cannellini beans
3¾ cups hot vegetable or chicken stock
2 teaspoons dried basil
½ cup dried porcini mushrooms, soaked for 10 minutes in enough warm water to cover
3 ounces vermicelli
3 tablespoons pesto
Freshly grated Parmesan cheese, for serving (optional)

Slice the eggplant into rings about ½ inch thick, then cut each ring into 4 pieces.

Cut the tomatoes and potato into small dice. Cut the carrot into sticks, about 1 inch long, and cut the leek into rings.

Place the cannellini beans and their liquid in a large pan. Add the eggplant, tomatoes, potatoes, carrot, and leek, stirring to mix.

Add the stock to the pan and bring to a boil. Reduce the heat and let simmer for 15 minutes.

Add the basil, dried mushrooms, their soaking liquid, and the vermicelli and simmer for 5 minutes or until all of the vegetables are tender.

Remove the pan from the heat and stir in the pesto.

Serve with the cheese, if using.

New England Clam Chowder

serves 6

- **1 cup water**
- **1 pound little neck clams, washed**
- **2 slices bacon, cut into ¼ inch pieces**
- **1 tablespoon butter**
- **½ yellow onion, diced**
- **2 tablespoons flour**
- **2 (10 ounce) cans whole clams, drained**
- **2 cups cold clam juice (Part of this may be made up from the drained canned clam liquid, but clam juice has a stronger clam flavor)**
- **1½ pounds (5 medium) Idaho potatoes, peeled, and cut into ¼ inch cubes**
- **1 cup whole milk**
- **1 cup cream**
- **Salt and freshly ground black pepper to taste**
- **Fresh chopped parsley to garnish**
- **Oyster crackers, to garnish**

Bring one cup of water to a boil in a small saucepan over high heat. Add the little neck clams, cover tightly, and cook for a couple minutes, until the clams open. Remove the clams to a bowl and reserve. Strain the cooking liquid and reserve.

In large saucepan, over medium heat, cook the bacon in the butter until almost crisp. Remove the bacon with slotted spoon and reserve, leaving the butter and rendered bacon fat in the pan.

Reduce the heat to medium-low, and add the onions. Sauté until soft and translucent, about 5 minutes. Add the flour and cook, stirring, for 2 minutes. Whisk in the cold clam juice, slowly at first. Add the reserved clam cooking liquid. Bring back to a simmer and add the potatoes. Cover and cook for 20 minutes, or until the potatoes are tender.

Note: At this point some chowder-heads like to smash some of the potatoes against the bottom of the pan with a masher to add body to the soup. Optional!

Stir in the canned clams, milk, and cream. Reduce heat to low, and cook until just heated through. Do not boil. Add the reserved little neck clams, and cook for another minute. Taste and season with salt and freshly ground black pepper as needed.

Serve hot topped with the reserved bacon, parsley, and oyster crackers.

Potato Skins with Guacamole

serves 4

4 x 8 ounce baking potatoes
2 teaspoons olive oil
Coarse sea salt and pepper
Chopped fresh chives, for garnish

Guacamole dip

1 cup ripe avocado, mashed
1 tablespoon lemon juice
2 ripe, firm tomatoes, finely chopped
1 teaspoon grated lemon rind
½ cup lowfat soft cheese with herbs and garlic
4 scallions, finely chopped
Few drops of Tabasco sauce
Salt and pepper

Bake the potatoes in a preheated oven, 400°F, for 1¼ hours. Remove from the oven and let cool for 30 minutes. Reset the oven to 425°F.

Halve the potatoes lengthwise and scoop out 2 tablespoons of the flesh.

Slice in half again. Place on a cookie sheet and lightly brush the flesh side with oil. Sprinkle with salt and pepper. Bake for an additional 25 minutes until golden and crisp.

To make the guacamole dip, mash the avocado with the lemon juice. Add the remaining ingredients and mix.

Drain the potato skins on paper towels and transfer to a warmed serving platter. Garnish with the chives. Pile the avocado mixture into a serving bowl.

Stuffed Mushrooms

serves 4

8 open-cap mushrooms
1 tablespoon olive oil
1 small leek, chopped
1 celery stalk, chopped
4 ounces firm bean curd, diced
1 zucchini, chopped
1 carrot, chopped
¾ cups whole wheat breadcrumbs
2 tablespoons chopped fresh basil
1 tablespoon tomato paste
2 tablespoons pine nuts
¾ cup grated cheddar cheese
⅔ cup vegetable stock
Pinch of salt
Freshly ground black pepper

Preheat the oven to 425°F.

Remove the stems from the mushrooms and chop finely. Reserve the caps.

Heat the olive oil in a large heavy skillet over medium heat. Add the mushroom stems, leek, celery, bean curd, zucchini, and carrot and cook, stirring continuously, for 3–4 minutes.

Stir in the breadcrumbs, basil, tomato paste, and pine nuts. Season with salt and pepper to taste and mix thoroughly.

Divide the stuffing mixture evenly among the mushroom caps and sprinkle the grated cheese over the top. Arrange the mushrooms in a shallow ovenproof dish and pour the stock around them.

Cook in the oven for 20 minutes or until the mushrooms are cooked through and the cheese has melted and browned. Remove the mushrooms from the dish and serve.

Chicken Noodle Soup

serves 6

For the broth

1 large whole chicken, about 4 to 5 pounds

Salt and freshly ground black pepper

1 carrot, chopped

1 rib celery, chopped

1 onion, chopped

1 clove garlic, peeled

4 sprigs thyme

1 bay leaf

1 whole clove

1 teaspoon ketchup

For the soup

1 tablespoon butter

1 onion, diced

2 large carrots, diced

2 sticks celery, diced

¼ teaspoon poultry seasoning

2 cups uncooked egg noodles, or other macaroni

1 tablespoon chopped parsley

Preheat oven to 450°F. Season the chicken inside and out with salt and pepper. Add the carrots, celery and onions to an oiled 9 x 13-inch roasting pan, and place the chicken on top. Roast for 60 minutes, or until a thermometer inserted in the thickest part of a thigh registers 160°F. Remove the chicken from the oven and allow to rest until cool enough to handle. Pull off the breast meat, and larger pieces of thigh and leg meat, and refrigerate until needed.

Transfer the chicken carcass and vegetables from the roasting pan into a large stockpot. Add 2 quarts of cold water, along with the garlic, thyme, bay leaf, clove, and ketchup. Bring to a boil, turn down heat to low, and simmer for 2 hours. The liquid level should remain about the same, so every so often add a splash of water to the pot.

While the broth is simmering, place a soup pot on medium-low heat. Melt the butter, and sauté the diced onion, carrots, and celery in the butter until they begin to soften, about 15 minutes. Stir in the poultry seasoning, turn off the heat, and reserve until the broth is done.

Skim the fat from the top of the broth, and strain it into the soup pot with the sautéed vegetables; bring to a boil. Turn down to low and simmer until the vegetables are tender. Taste, and add salt and fresh ground black pepper to taste. Turn heat up to high, add the egg noodles and boil for 7 minutes. Dice the chicken and add to the pot. Turn heat down to medium and simmer until the noodles are tender. Stir in the parsley, and serve.

Vegetable Cake

serves 4

Base

2 tablespoons vegetable oil, plus extra for brushing

2 pounds 12 ounces waxy potatoes, sliced

Topping

1 tablespoon vegetable oil

1 leek, chopped

1 zucchini, grated

1 red bell pepper, seeded and diced

1 green bell pepper, seeded and diced

1 carrot, grated

2 teaspoons chopped fresh parsley

8 ounces soft cheese

4 tablespoons grated sharp cheese

2 eggs, beaten

Salt and pepper

Shredded cooked leek, for garnish

Salad, for serving

Preheat oven to 375°.

Brush an 8-inch spring form cake pan with oil.

To make the base, heat the oil in a skillet. Cook the potato slices until softened and browned. Drain on paper towels and place in the bottom of the prepared cake pan.

To make the topping, heat the oil in a separate skillet. Add the leek and cook over low heat, stirring frequently, for 3–4 minutes until softened. Add the zucchini, bell peppers, carrot, and parsley to the skillet and cook over low heat for 5–7 minutes or until the vegetables have softened.

Meanwhile, beat the cheeses and eggs together in a bowl. Stir in the vegetables and season with salt and pepper to taste. Spoon the mixture evenly over the potato base. Cook for 20–25 minutes until the cake is set.

Remove the vegetable cake from the pan, transfer to a warmed serving plate, garnish with the shredded leek, and serve with a crisp salad.

Crab Cakes with Salsa Verde

serves 4-5

14 ounces crabmeat

5 pieces (9 ounces) white fish fillet, skinned and chopped ie) Seabass, cod or flounder

1 fresh red chile, seeded and chopped

1 garlic clove, chopped

1-inch piece of fresh gingerroot, chopped

1 lemongrass stalk, chopped

3 tablespoons chopped fresh cilantro

1 egg white

vegetable oil, for frying

Salsa verde

2 fresh green chiles, seeded and chopped

8 scallions, chopped

2 garlic cloves, chopped

1 bunch of fresh parsley

grated rind and juice of 1 lime

juice of 1 lemon

4 tablespoons olive oil

1 tablespoon green Tabasco sauce

Pinch of salt

Freshly ground black pepper

Place the crabmeat, fish, red chile, garlic, ginger, lemongrass, cilantro, and egg white in a food processor and process until thoroughly blended, then transfer to a bowl, cover with plastic wrap, and let chill in the refrigerator for 30–60 minutes.

Meanwhile, make the salsa verde. Put the green chiles, scallions, garlic, and parsley in a food processor and process until finely chopped. Transfer to a small bowl and stir in the lime rind, lime and lemon juice, olive oil, and green Tabasco sauce. Season with salt and pepper to taste, cover with plastic wrap, and let chill in the refrigerator until ready to serve.

Heat 2 tablespoons of oil in a nonstick skillet. Add spoonfuls of the crab mixture, flattening them gently with a spatula and keeping them spaced well apart. Cook for 4 minutes, then turn with a spatula and cook the other side for 3 minutes, or until golden brown. Remove from the skillet and keep warm while you cook the remaining batches, adding more oil if necessary. Transfer the crab cakes to a large serving plate and serve with the salsa verde.

Shrimp Cocktail

serves 4-6

2 pounds jumbo shrimp deveined, but unpeeled

1 lemon cut in wedges

1 cup prepared cocktail sauce

For the poaching liquid

3 quarts cold water

½ onion, sliced

2 garlic cloves, peeled and bruised

2 springs tarragon

1 bay leaf

1 tablespoon Old Bay seasoning

½ lemon, juiced

1 teaspoon black peppercorns

For the cocktail sauce

½ cup ketchup

¼ cup chili sauce

¼ cup horseradish, or to taste

1 teaspoon fresh lemon juice

1 teaspoon Worcestershire sauce

Dash of hot sauce, optional

Pinch of salt

Frozen shrimp are now commonly available deveined (meaning the intestinal tract removed), but with the shell on. This style makes the best shrimp cocktail since the shell adds flavor when they are poached.

If you can't find this type, get shell-on shrimp and use a pair of scissors to make a cut through the shell, down the back of the shrimp. Then use a small sharp knife to make ⅛ inch deep incision and remove the intestinal tract. Rinse under cold water.

Add all the poaching liquid ingredients to a large stockpot. Place over high heat and bring to a simmer. Turn the heat down to low and simmer for 30 minutes.

Fill a mixing bowl with ice water and set aside. Turn the heat under the poaching liquid to high, and bring to a boil. Add the shrimp and boil for 5 minutes or until cooked through. Transfer the shrimp into the ice water. When cold, drain well, and serve with cocktail sauce and lemon wedges.

The shrimp can be served as is (also known as "peel and eat"), or for a "fancier" presentation, peel for your guests ahead of time and arrange around the rim of a cocktail glass.

For the sauce (makes 1 cup): Combine all ingredients in a small bowl, mix thoroughly, and refrigerate for at least one hour before serving.

Cobb Salad

serves 4

8 slices bacon

4 large handfuls mixed baby greens, torn into bite-size pieces

3 hard-boiled eggs, peeled, chopped

1 pound cooked chicken, cubed

2 avocados, peeled, pitted, cubed

1 cup cherry tomatoes, halved

¾ cup Roquefort cheese, crumbled

½ teaspoon Dijon mustard

¼ cup red wine vinegar

1 teaspoon Worcestershire sauce

1 clove garlic, crushed into a paste

¼ teaspoon salt

¼ teaspoon fresh ground black pepper

⅓ cup olive oil

Cook the bacon until crisp, drain on paper towels, and when cool enough to handle, crumble and set aside.

Arrange a bed of lettuce in shallow bowls. Arrange the eggs, bacon, chicken, avocados, tomatoes, and Roquefort cheese in rows on top of the lettuce, covering the surface completely.

In a bowl, whisk together the mustard, vinegar, Worcestershire, garlic, salt, and pepper.

Slowly drizzle in the olive oil, whisking constantly, to form the dressing.

Drizzle the dressing evenly over the salad, and serve immediately.

Tomato & Cheese Bruschetta

serves 4

8 slices sourdough bread

4 garlic cloves, crushed

2 tablespoons butter

1 tablespoon chopped basil

4 large, ripe tomatoes

1 tablespoon tomato paste

8 pitted black olives, halved

⅓ cup mozzarella cheese, sliced

Pinch of salt

Freshly ground black pepper

Fresh basil leaves, for garnish

Dressing

1 tablespoon extra virgin olive oil

2 teaspoons lemon juice

1 teaspoon clear honey

Cut the sour dough bread into slices Toast under a hot broiler for 2–3 minutes until golden.

Beat the garlic, butter, and basil together and spread evenly onto each slice.

Cut a cross shape at the top of each tomato. Plunge the tomatoes into a bowl of boiling water—this will make the skin easier to peel. After a few minutes, pick each tomato up with a fork and peel off the skin. Chop the tomato flesh and mix with the tomato paste and olives. Divide the mixture among the slices of toast.

Mix the dressing ingredients and drizzle over the toast. Arrange the mozzarella on top and season with salt and pepper to taste.

Return the toast to the broiler for 1–2 minutes until the cheese has melted. Serve, garnished with basil leaves.

Pork & Vegetable Broth

serves 4

1 tablespoon vegetable oil or chili oil

1 garlic clove, chopped

3 scallions, trimmed and sliced

1 red bell pepper, seeded and finely sliced

2 tablespoons cornstarch

4 cups vegetable broth

1 tablespoon soy sauce

2 tablespoons rice wine or dry sherry

6 ounces pork tenderloin, sliced

1 tablespoon finely chopped lemongrass

1 small red chile, seeded and finely chopped

1 tablespoon grated fresh ginger

Salt and freshly ground pepper, to taste

4 ounces fine egg noodles

1 cup water

¾ cup canned water chestnuts, drained and sliced

Heat the oil in a large pan. Add the garlic and scallions and cook over medium heat, stirring, for 3 minutes, until slightly softened. Add the bell pepper and cook for an additional 5 minutes, stirring.

In a bowl, mix the cornstarch with enough of the stock to make a smooth paste and stir it into the pan. Cook, stirring, for 2 minutes. Stir in the remaining stock, the soy sauce, and rice wine, then add the pork, lemongrass, chile, and ginger. Season with salt and pepper to taste. Bring to a boil, then lower the heat and simmer for 25 minutes.

In a separate pan, bring the water to a boil; add the noodles, and cook for 3 minutes, or according to the package directions. Remove from the heat, drain, then add the noodles to the soup along with the water chestnuts. Cook for another 2 minutes, then remove from the heat and ladle into serving bowls. Serve immediately.

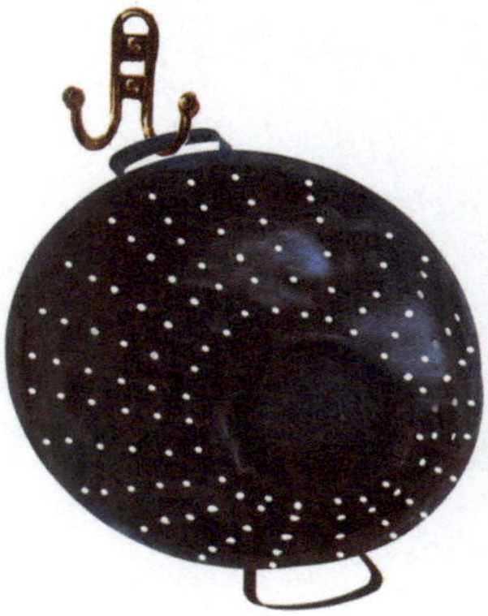

Baked Potatoes with Beans

serves 6

4 pounds russet potatoes

4 tablespoons vegetable oil

1 large onion, chopped

2 garlic cloves, crushed

1 teaspoon ground turmeric

1 tablespoon cumin seeds

2 tablespoons mild curry paste

One 14.5 ounce can of tomatoes, chopped

One 15 ounce can black-eyed peas, drained and rinsed

One 15 ounce can red kidney beans, drained and rinsed

1 tablespoon lemon juice

2 tablespoons tomato paste

2/3 cup water

2 tablespoons chopped fresh mint or cilantro

Pinch of salt

Freshly ground black pepper

Preheat the oven to 350F.

Scrub the potatoes and prick several times with a fork. Place the potatoes in a roasting pan and cook for 1–11/4 hours, or until the potatoes feel soft when gently squeezed.

About 20 minutes before the end of cooking time, prepare the topping. Heat the oil in a pan, then add the onion and cook over low heat, stirring frequently, for 5 minutes. Add the garlic, turmeric, cumin seeds, and curry paste and cook gently for 1 minute.

Stir in the tomatoes, black-eyed peas, red kidney beans, lemon juice, tomato paste, water, and chopped mint. Season with salt and pepper to taste, then cover and simmer over low heat, stirring frequently, for 10 minutes.

When the potatoes are cooked, cut them in half and mash the flesh lightly with a fork. Spoon the prepared bean mixture on top. Place on warmed serving plates and serve immediately.

Niçoise Pasta Salad

serves 4

12 ounces dried conchiglie (pasta shells)

1 cup green beans

¼ cup canned anchovy fillets, drained

2 tablespoons whole milk

2 small heads of crisp lettuce, such as romaine

3 large tomatoes

4 hard-boiled eggs

One 5-ounce can tuna, packed in oil

1 cup pitted black olives

Salt

Vinaigrette

¼ cup extra virgin olive oil

2 tablespoons white wine vinegar

1 teaspoon whole-grain mustard

Pinch of salt

Freshly ground black pepper

Bring a large pan of lightly salted water to a boil over medium heat. Add the pasta and cook for 8–10 minutes, or according to the package directions, until tender but still firm to the bite. Drain the pasta thoroughly and refresh in cold water.

Bring a small pan of lightly salted water to a boil over medium heat. Add the beans and cook for 5 minutes, or until done. Drain thoroughly and refresh in cold water, then drain again and set aside.

Put the anchovies into a shallow bowl, then pour over the milk and set aside for 10 minutes. Meanwhile, tear the lettuce into large pieces. Blanch the tomatoes in boiling water for 1–2 minutes, then drain. Skin and coarsely chop the flesh. Shell the eggs and cut into quarters. Flake the tuna into large chunks.

Drain the anchovies and the pasta. Put all the salad ingredients into a large bowl and gently mix together.

To make the vinaigrette: Beat the oil, vinegar, and mustard together, season to taste with salt and pepper, and keep in the refrigerator until ready to serve. Just before serving, pour the vinaigrette over the salad.

Turkey & Lentil Soup

serves 4

1 tablespoon olive oil
1 garlic clove, chopped
1 large onion, chopped
4 cups mushrooms, sliced
1 red bell pepper, seeded and chopped
6 tomatoes, peeled, seeded, and chopped
4 cups chicken stock
⅔ cup red wine
⅔ cup cauliflower florets
1 carrot, chopped
1 cup red lentils
Salt and freshly ground pepper, to taste
One pound 4 ounces chopped, cooked turkey
1 zucchini, chopped
1 tablespoon shredded fresh basil, plus extra sprigs to garnish

Heat the oil in a large pan. Add the garlic and onion and cook over medium heat, stirring, for 3 minutes, until slightly softened. Add the mushrooms, bell pepper, and tomatoes, and cook for another 5 minutes, stirring.

Pour in the stock and red wine, then add the cauliflower, carrot, and red lentils. Season to taste with salt and pepper.

Bring to a boil, then lower the heat and simmer for 25 minutes, until the vegetables are tender and cooked through.

Add the turkey and zucchini to the pan and cook for 10 minutes. Stir in the shredded basil and cook for another 5 minutes, then remove from the heat and ladle into serving bowls. Garnish with fresh basil and serve immediately.

Hash Browns with Tomato Sauce

serves 4

1 pound waxy potatoes
1 carrot, diced
1 celery stalk, diced
¾ cups diced white mushrooms
1 onion, diced
2 garlic cloves, crushed
⅓ cup frozen peas, thawed
1 cup freshly grated Parmesan cheese
4 tablespoons vegetable oil
2 tablespoons butter
Pinch of salt
Freshly ground black pepper

Sauce

1¼ cups strained tomatoes
2 tablespoons chopped fresh cilantro
1 tablespoon soy sauce
½ teaspoon chili powder
2 teaspoons brown sugar
2 teaspoons mild mustard
5 tablespoons vegetable stock

Bring a pan of lightly salted water to a boil and cook the potatoes for 10 minutes. Drain and set aside to cool. Meanwhile, bring another pan of lightly salted water to a boil and cook the carrot for 5 minutes.

When the potatoes are cool enough to handle, grate them with a coarse grater.

Drain the carrot and add it to the grated potatoes, with the celery, mushrooms, onion, garlic, peas, and cheese. Season with salt and pepper to taste.

Put all of the sauce ingredients into a small pan and bring to a boil. Reduce the heat to low and simmer for 15 minutes.

Divide the potato mixture into 8 equal-size portions and shape into flattened rectangles with your hands.

Heat the oil and butter in a skillet and cook the hash browns in batches over low heat for 4–5 minutes on each side, until crisp and golden brown.

Transfer the hash browns to a warmed serving plate and serve immediately with the tomato sauce.

Sweet Potato Patties

serves 4

1 pound 2 ounces sweet potatoes

2 garlic cloves, crushed

1 small fresh green chile, chopped

2 sprigs of fresh cilantro, chopped

1 tablespoon dark soy sauce

All-purpose flour, for shaping

Vegetable oil, for frying

Sesame seeds, for sprinkling

Soy-tomato sauce

2 teaspoons vegetable oil

1 garlic clove, finely chopped

1½ teaspoons finely chopped fresh gingerroot

3 tomatoes, peeled and chopped

2 tablespoons dark soy sauce

1 tablespoon lime juice

2 tablespoons chopped fresh cilantro

To make the soy-tomato sauce, heat the oil in a wok and stir-fry the garlic and ginger for about 1 minute. Add the tomatoes and stir-fry for an additional 2 minutes. Remove from the heat and stir in the soy sauce, lime juice, and chopped cilantro. Set aside and keep warm.

Peel the sweet potatoes and grate finely (you can do this with a food processor). Place the garlic, chile, and cilantro in a mortar and crush to a smooth paste with a pestle. Stir in the soy sauce and mix with the sweet potatoes.

Divide the mixture into 12 equal portions. Dip into flour and pat into a flat, round patty shape.

Heat a shallow layer of oil in a wide skillet. Cook the sweet potato patties in batches over high heat until golden, turning once.

Drain on paper towels and sprinkle with the sesame seeds. Serve hot, with a spoonful of the soy-tomato sauce.

3

Grandma's Family Meals

Whole Roast Garlic Herb Chicken with Pan Gravy

serves 4

1 large whole chicken, about 5 pounds, rinsed, dried with paper towels

4 cloves garlic

⅓ cup olive oil

2 teaspoons very finely minced fresh thyme leaves

2 teaspoons very finely minced fresh rosemary leaves

1 teaspoon dried Italian herbs

Salt and freshly ground black pepper to taste

For the gravy

1½ tablespoons reserved chicken fat

1 tablespoon butter

1 heaping tablespoon flour

2 cups cold chicken broth

½ teaspoon balsamic vinegar

4 sprigs fresh thyme

Salt and freshly ground black pepper to taste

Pre-heat oven to 450°F.

Remove skins and crush the garlic cloves with the flat of a knife. Mince and and press until it is a very fine paste.

Add olive oil, garlic, thyme, rosemary and dried Italian herbs to a large mixing bowl. Rub the chicken inside and out with the mixture. Continue or leave to marinade overnight or for a few hours.

Place chicken in an oven-proof skillet or roasting pan. Something that can be used on the stove flame later. Season the cavity with salt and freshly ground black pepper. Truss the legs with kitchen string.

Place in the centre of the oven and roast for one hour or until a thermometer registers 165°F. Remove the chicken, place on a platter and cover with foil. Allow to rest while making the gravy.

Pour the excess chicken fat from the pan, leaving 1½ tablespoons behind, Place back on the stove and add the butter. When the butter melts add a little flour and cook, stirring with a whisk constantly until golden brown. Whisk in 2 cups of cold chicken broth, balsamic vinegar and thyme. Turn the heat to high, and boil for 5 minutes stirring until the gravy is thickened.

Grandma's Meatloaf

serves 6-8

3 cloves garlic, peeled
1 large carrot, diced
1 stick celery. diced
1 yellow onion, diced
1 red bell pepper, diced
4 large white mushrooms, sliced
1 tablespoon olive oil
2 tablespoons butter
1 teaspoon dried thyme
2 teaspoons finely minced fresh rosemary
1 teaspoon Worcestershire sauce
¼ cup ketchup
½ teaspoon cayenne
2½ pounds ground chuck steak
2 teaspoons salt
1 teaspoon black pepper
2 eggs, beaten
1 cup plain bread crumbs

For the glaze

2 tablespoons brown sugar
2 tablespoons ketchup
1 tablespoon Dijon mustard
Pinch of salt

Pre-heat oven to 325°F. Add the garlic, carrot, celery, onion, red bell pepper, and white mushrooms into a food processor. Pulse on and off until the vegetables are very finely minced.

Add the butter and olive oil to a large skillet and fry over a medium heat. When the butter melts, add the vegetable mixture and cook, stirring, about 10 minutes.

Remove from the heat and stir in the thyme, rosemary, Worcestershire, ketchup, and cayenne pepper. Set aside and let cool to room temperature.

Add the ground beef to a large mixing bowl. Very gently break up the meat with your fingertips. Pour in the cooled vegetable mixture, salt, black pepper, and eggs. Add the breadcrumbs and continue mixing until combined.

Lightly grease a shallow roasting pan. Place the meatloaf mixture in the center. Wet your hands with cold water and form into a loaf shape; about 6 inches wide, by 4 inches high. Place in the center of the preheated oven and set the timer for 30 minutes.

To make the glaze, whisk together the brown sugar, ketchup, Dijon, and pinch of salt in a small bowl to make the glaze. After 30 minutes, remove the meatloaf and evenly spread the glaze over the top with a spoon.

Return to the oven for about 35 to 45 minutes, Remove and let rest for at least 15 minutes before slicing and serving.

Orange Turkey with Rice

serves 4

1 tablespoon olive oil
1 medium onion, chopped
1 pound skinless lean turkey, cut into thin strips
1¼ cups unsweetened orange juice
1 bay leaf
1½ cups small broccoli florets
1 large zucchini, diced
1 large orange
3 pounds cooked brown rice
Salt and pepper
Tomato and onion salad, to serve
9–10 pitted black olives in brine, drained and quartered, to garnish
Shredded basil leaves, to garnish

Heat the oil in a large skillet and cook the onion and turkey, stirring, for 4–5 minutes, until lightly browned.

Pour in the orange juice and add the bay leaf and seasoning. Bring to a boil and simmer for 10 minutes.

Meanwhile, bring a large pan of water to a boil and cook the broccoli florets, covered, for 2 minutes. Add the diced zucchini, then bring back to a boil. Cover and cook for another 3 minutes. Drain and set aside.

Using a sharp knife, peel off the skin and white pith from the orange. Slice down the orange to make thin circular slices, then halve each slice.

Stir the broccoli, zucchini, rice, and orange slices into the turkey mixture. Gently mix together and season, then heat through for another 3–4 minutes, or until the mixture is piping hot.

Transfer the turkey rice to warm serving plates and garnish with black olives and shredded basil leaves. Serve with a fresh tomato and onion salad.

Macaroni & Tuna Layer

serves 4

10 ounces dried macaroni

2 tablespoon oil

1 garlic clove, crushed

1 cup white mushrooms, sliced

½ red bell pepper, thinly sliced

One 5 ounce can tuna in brine, drained and flaked

½ teaspoon dried oregano

Salt and pepper

Sauce

2 tablespoons butter or margarine

1 tablespoon all-purpose flour

1 cup whole milk

2 tomatoes, sliced

2 tablespoons dried breadcrumbs

⅓ cup sharp cheddar or Parmesan cheese, grated

Preheat the oven to 400°F.

Bring a large pan of lightly salted water to a boil and cook the macaroni, with 1 tablespoon of the oil added, for 10–12 minutes or until tender. Drain, rinse, and drain thoroughly.

Heat the remaining oil in a pan or skillet and fry the garlic, mushrooms, and bell pepper until soft. Add the tuna, oregano, and seasoning and heat through.

Grease a 4-cup ovenproof dish and add half of the cooked macaroni. Cover with the tuna mixture and then add the remaining macaroni.

To make the sauce, melt the butter in a pan, stir in the flour and cook for 1 minute. Add the milk gradually and bring to a boil. Simmer for 1–2 minutes, stirring continuously, until thickened. Season to taste. Pour the sauce over the macaroni.

Lay the sliced tomatoes over the sauce and sprinkle with the breadcrumbs and cheese.

Bake for 25 minutes, or until piping hot and the top is well browned.

Classic Beef Fajitas

serves 4-8

1 pounds 8 ounces beef tenderloin, cut into strips

6 garlic cloves, chopped

juice of 1 lime

Pinch of mild chili powder

Pinch of paprika

Pinch of ground cumin

Salt and pepper

1–2 tablespoons vegetable oil, for frying

For serving

12 flour tortillas

1–2 avocados, pitted, peeled, sliced, and tossed with lime juice

½ cup sour cream

Pico de galla salsa

8 ripe tomatoes, diced

3 scallions, sliced

1–2 fresh green chiles, such as jalapeño or serrano, seeded and chopped

3–4 tablespoons chopped fresh cilantro

5–8 radishes, diced

Ground cumin

Salt and pepper

Combine the beef with half the garlic, half the lime juice, the chili powder, paprika, cumin, and oil. Add salt and pepper, mix well, and marinate for at least 30 minutes at room temperature or overnight in the refrigerator.

To make the pico de gallo salsa, put the tomatoes in a bowl with the scallions, chiles cilantro, and radishes. Season with cumin and salt and pepper to taste. Set aside.

Heat the tortillas in a lightly greased nonstick skillet. Wrap them in foil, as you work, to keep them warm.

Stir-fry the meat in a little oil over high heat until browned and just cooked through.

Serve the sizzling hot meat with the warmed tortillas, the pico de gallo salsa, avocado, and sour cream for each person to make his or her own rolled up fajitas.

Sausage & Bean Casserole

serves 4

8 Italian sausages
3 tablespoons olive oil
1 large onion, chopped
2 garlic cloves, chopped
1 green bell pepper, seeded and sliced
One 14.5 ounce can chopped tomatoes
2 tablespoons sun-dried tomato paste
One 14.5 ounce can cannelloni beans
Mashed potatoes or rice, to serve

Prick the sausages all over with a fork. Heat 2 tablespoons of the oil in a large, heavy-bottom skillet. Add the sausages and cook over low heat, turning frequently, for 10–15 minutes, until evenly browned and cooked through. Remove them from the skillet and keep warm. Drain off the oil and wipe out the skillet with paper towels.

Heat the remaining oil in the skillet. Add the onion, garlic, and bell pepper to the skillet and cook for 5 minutes, stirring occasionally, or until softened.

Add the tomatoes to the skillet and let the mixture simmer for about 5 minutes, stirring occasionally, or until slightly reduced and thickened.

Stir the sun-dried tomato paste, cannellini beans, and Italian sausages into the mixture in the skillet. Cook for 4–5 minutes or until the mixture is piping hot. Add 4–5 tablespoons of water if the mixture becomes too dry during cooking.

Transfer the sausage and bean casserole to serving plates and serve with mashed potatoes.

Fried Chicken with Tomato & Bacon Sauce

serves 4

2 tablespoons butter

2 tablespoons olive oil

4 skinless, boneless chicken breasts or 8 skinless, boneless chicken thighs

Tomato & bacon sauce

2 tablespoons butter

2 tablespoons olive oil

1 large onion, finely chopped

2 garlic cloves, finely chopped

1 celery stalk, finely chopped

4 slices bacon, chopped

One 14.5 ounce can chopped tomatoes

2 tablespoons tomato paste

Brown sugar, to taste

½ cup water

1 tablespoon chopped fresh basil

1 tablespoon chopped fresh parsley, plus extra to garnish

Salt and pepper

First, make the sauce. Melt the butter with the oil in a large pan. Add the onion, garlic, celery, and bacon and cook over low heat, stirring occasionally, for 5 minutes, until softened. Stir in the tomatoes, tomato paste, sugar to taste, and water and season with salt and pepper. Increase the heat to medium and bring to a boil, then reduce the heat and simmer, stirring occasionally, for 15–20 minutes, until thickened.

Meanwhile, melt the butter with the oil in a large skillet. Add the chicken and cook over medium– high heat for 4–5 minutes on each side, until evenly browned.

Stir the basil and parsley into the sauce. Add the chicken and spoon the sauce over it. Cover and simmer for 10–15 minutes, until cooked through and tender. Garnish with parsley and serve immediately.

Fish Baked with Lime

serves 4

2 pounds white fish fillets, such as sea bass or cod
1 lime, halved
3 tablespoons extra-virgin olive oil
1 large onion, finely chopped
3 garlic cloves, finely chopped
3 pickled jalapeno chiles chopped
6 tablespoons chopped fresh cilantro
Pinch of salt
Freshly ground black pepper
Lemon and lime wedges, for serving

Preheat the oven to 350°F.

Place the fish fillets in a bowl and sprinkle with salt and pepper. Squeeze the juice from the lime over the fish.

Heat the olive oil in a skillet. Add the onion and garlic and cook for about 2 minutes, stirring frequently, until softened. Remove from the heat.

Place a third of the onion mixture and a little of the chiles and cilantro in the bottom of a shallow casserole or roasting pan. Arrange the fish on top. Top with the remaining onion mixture, chiles, and cilantro.

Bake for 15–20 minutes or until the fish has become slightly opaque and firm to the touch. Serve immediately, with the lemon and lime wedges for squeezing over the fish.

Pork Chops and Spicy Beans

serves 4

3 tablespoons vegetable oil

4 lean pork chops

2 onions, peeled and thinly sliced

2 garlic cloves, peeled and crushed

2 fresh green chiles, seeded and chopped

1-in piece of fresh gingerroot, peeled and chopped

1½ teaspoons cumin seeds

1½ teaspoons ground coriander

2½ cups stock or water

2 tablespoons tomato paste

½ eggplant, trimmed and cut into ½-inch dice

Pinch of salt

Freshly ground black pepper

One 15-ounce can red kidney beans, drained

4 tablespoons heavy cream

Heat the oil in a large skillet, add the pork chops, and fry until sealed and browned on both sides. Remove from the skillet and set aside until required.

Add the onions, garlic, chii, ginger, and spices and fry gently for 2 minutes. Stir in the stock, tomato paste, and eggplant and season with salt and pepper.

Bring the mixture to a boil, place the pork chops on top, then cover and simmer gently over medium heat for 30 minutes.

Remove the chops for a moment and stir the red kidney beans and heavy cream into the mixture. Return the chops to the skillet, cover, and heat through gently for 5 minutes.

Taste and adjust the seasoning, if necessary. Serve hot.

Vegetable Lasagna

serves 4

1 eggplant, sliced
3 tablespoons olive oil
2 garlic cloves, crushed
1 red onion, sliced
3 mixed bell peppers, seeded and diced
2 cups sliced mixed mushrooms
2 celery stalks, sliced
1 zucchini, diced
½ teaspoon chili powder
½ teaspoon ground cumin
2 tomatoes, chopped
1¼ cups canned tomatoes
2 tablespoons chopped fresh basil
8 no-precook lasagna Verdi sheets
salt and pepper

Cheese sauce

2 tablespoons butter or margarine
1 tablespoon all-purpose flour
½ cup vegetable stock
1¼ cups milk
¾ cup grated cheddar cheese
1 teaspoon Dijon mustard
1 tablespoon chopped fresh basil
1 egg, beaten

Preheat the oven to 350°F.

Place the eggplant slices in a colander, sprinkle with salt, and let stand for 20 minutes. Rinse under cold water, drain, and reserve.

Heat the oil in a saucepan. Add the garlic and onion and sauté for 1–2 minutes. Add the bell peppers, mushrooms, celery, and zucchini and cook, stirring constantly, for 3–4 minutes. Stir in the chili powder and cumin and cook for 1 minute. Mix in the tomatoes, strained canned tomatoes, and basil, and season to taste with salt and pepper.

For the cheese sauce, melt the butter in a saucepan. Stir in the flour and cook for 1 minute. Remove from the heat and gradually stir in the stock and milk. Return to the heat, then add half the cheese and the mustard. Boil, stirring, until thickened. Stir in the basil. Remove from the heat and stir in the egg.

Place half the lasagna sheets in a rectangular, ovenproof dish. Top with half the vegetable mixture and half the eggplant slices. Repeat the layers, then spoon the cheese sauce on top. Sprinkle with the remaining cheese and bake in the preheated oven for 40 minutes, or until golden. Serve immediately.

Cured Ham Cooked in Cider

serves 6

2 pounds boneless cured ham in a single piece
1 onion, halved
4 cloves
6 black peppercorns
1 teaspoon juniper berries (optional)
1 celery rib, chopped
1 carrot, sliced
3 cups cider or unsweetened apple juice

Place a rack in the slow cooker, and stand the ham on it. Stud each of the onion halves with 2 cloves and add to the cooker with the peppercorns, juniper berries, celery, and carrot.

Pour in the hard cider or apple juice, cover, and cook on low for 8 hours until the meat is tender.

Remove the ham from the cooker and place on a board. Tent with foil and let stand for 10–15 minutes. Discard the cooking liquid and flavorings.

Cut off any rind and fat from the ham, then carve into slices, and serve with cooked vegetables.

Spaghetti with Meat Sauce

serves 4

1 tablespoon olive oil
1 onion, finely chopped
2 garlic cloves, chopped
1 carrot, scraped and chopped
1 celery rib, chopped
2 ounces pancetta, diced
12 ounces lean ground beef
One 14.5-ounce can chopped tomatoes
2 teaspoons dried oregano
½ cup red wine
2 tablespoons tomato paste
Salt and freshly ground black pepper
1 pound 8 ounces fresh spaghetti
Freshly grated Parmesan cheese, to serve

Heat the oil in a large skillet. Add the onions and cook for 3 minutes. Add the garlic, carrot, celery, and pancetta and sauté for 3–4 minutes or until the vegetables and pancetta are soft and are just beginning to brown.

Add the ground beef and cook, stirring, over high heat for another 3 minutes or until all of the meat is browned. Stir in the tomatoes, oregano, and wine and bring to a boil. Reduce the heat and let simmer for about 45 minutes. Stir in the tomato paste and season to taste with salt and pepper.

Cook the spaghetti in a pan of boiling salted water for 8–10 minutes until tender, but still has "bite." Drain thoroughly.

Transfer the spaghetti to a serving plate and pour the Bolognese sauce over the pasta. Toss to mix well and serve hot with the freshly grated Parmesan cheese.

Chicken with Black-Eyed Peas

serves 4

1 cup dried black-eyed peas, soaked overnight and drained

1 teaspoon salt

2 onions, finely chopped

2 garlic cloves, minced

1 teaspoon ground turmeric

1 teaspoon ground cumin

2 pounds 12 ounces chicken, cut into 8 pieces

1 green bell pepper, seeded and chopped

2 tablespoons olive oil

1-inch piece of fresh gingerroot, grated

2 teaspoons coriander seeds

½ teaspoon fennel seeds

1 tablespoon chopped fresh cilantro, for garnish

Put the black-eyed peas into a wok or large pan with the salt, onions, garlic, turmeric, and cumin. Cover the peas with water, bring to a boil, and cook for 15 minutes.

Add the chicken and bell pepper to the wok and bring to a boil. Reduce the heat and let simmer for 30 minutes until the peas are tender and the chicken juices run clear when the thickest parts of the pieces are pierced with the point of a sharp knife.

Heat the oil in a wok or pan and stir-fry the ginger, coriander seeds, and fennel seeds for 30 seconds.

Stir the fried spices into the chicken. Let simmer for an additional 5 minutes, garnish with the chopped cilantro, and serve immediately.

Slow Cooked Salmon

serves 4

⅔ cup fish stock

1 cup dry white wine

2 lemons

1 onion, thinly sliced

4 salmon fillets, about 6 ounces each

1 tablespoon dried mixed herbs

3 pounds spinach, coarse stalks removed

freshly grated nutmeg, to taste

¾ cup (1½ sticks) unsalted butter, plus extra for greasing

Salt and pepper

Lightly grease a slow cooker pot with butter. Pour the stock and wine into a pan and bring to a boil. Meanwhile, thinly slice 1 of the lemons. Put half the lemon slices and all the onion slices over the bottom of the slow cooker pot and top with the salmon fillets. Season to taste with salt and pepper, add the mixed herbs, and cover the fish with the remaining lemon slices. Pour the hot stock mixture over the fish, cover, and cook on low for 1½ hours, until the fish flakes easily.

Meanwhile, grate the rind and squeeze the juice from the remaining lemon. When the fish is nearly ready, cook the spinach, in just the water clinging to the leaves after washing, for 3–5 minutes, until wilted. Drain well, squeezing out as much water as possible. Chop finely, arrange on warmed individual plates, and season to taste with salt, pepper, and nutmeg.

Carefully lift the fish out of the slow cooker and discard the lemon slices, onion slices. Put the salmon fillets on top of the spinach and keep warm.

Melt the butter in a pan over low heat. Stir in the lemon rind and half the juice. Taste and adjust the seasoning, adding more lemon juice, salt, and pepper if needed. Pour the lemon butter sauce over the fish and serve immediately.

Roast Pork Tenderloin with Black Cherry Sauce

serves 6

2 trimmed pork tenderloins (about 1½ pounds each)

Kosher salt to taste

¼ cup coarsely ground black pepper

2 tablespoons vegetable oil

1 clove garlic, crushed

⅓ cup balsamic vinegar

½ cup black cherry preserves

1 cup chicken stock

2 tablespoons cold unsalted butter

Pre-heat oven to 375°F.

Coat all sides of the pork tenderloins generously with salt and black pepper, and to taste. Heat the vegetable oil, in a large, ovenproof frying pan, over medium-high heat, until it begins to smoke. Sear the pork on all sides, about 2 minutes per side. Turn off the heat; place the pan in the center of the preheated oven.

Roast the pork for about 25 minutes, or until the internal temperature reaches 140°F. When the pork is cooked, remove it from the pan to a plate and cover loosely with foil to rest while the sauce is made.

Pour off the excess fat from the frying pan, and place over high heat. Add the garlic and cook for just 15 seconds, then add the vinegar, cherry preserves, and chicken stock. Cook, scraping the bottom of the pan with a wooden spoon to deglaze the pan drippings.

Boil until the sauce reduces by about half, about 6 to 7 minutes. Turn off the heat, and whisk in the cold butter, stirring constantly until the butter disappears. Taste for salt, and adjust the seasoning. Slice the pork and serve with the sauce spooned over.

New York Strip Steak & Mushrooms

serves 4

For the mushroom salad

¼ cup olive oil

2 tablespoons butter

2 pounds large button mushrooms, thickly sliced

3 tablespoons sherry vinegar

2 garlic cloves, minced fine

1 tablespoon fresh chopped tarragon

Salt and fresh ground black pepper to taste

For the steaks

4 thick-cut (10 ounces) New York strip steaks

Salt and coarse-ground black pepper to taste

1 tablespoon vegetable oil

¼ cup chicken broth

1 tablespoon butter

To make the mushroom salad, melt the butter in the olive oil, in a large frying pan, over medium-high heat. When the butter starts to sizzle, add the mushrooms and cook, stirring, for 10 to 15 minutes, or until the mushroom juices have evaporated, and they're very well browned. Stir in the garlic, and cook for 2 minutes.

Pour in the vinegar, and as soon as it starts to boil, turn off the heat. Transfer into a bowl, and allow to cool to room temperature. Add the tarragon, salt, and freshly ground black pepper to taste. Reserve until needed.

Season the steaks generously on both sides with salt and coarse-ground black pepper. Place a large heavy skillet over medium-high heat. Add the oil, and when hot, sear the steaks for about 5 to 6 minutes per side for medium-rare. Remove to a plate to rest.

Turn up the heat and add the mushrooms. Add the broth and use a wooden spoon to scrape the bottom of the pan. Once the broth has deglazed the caramelized meat juices from the bottom of the pan, add the butter and stir until it disappears. Turn up the heat and add the mushrooms mix to mixture. Stir to combine. Taste and adjust seasoning.

Place the steaks on warm plates and spoon over the warm mushrooms. Serve immediately.

Meatballs with Tomato Relish

serves 4

1 onion, finely chopped

2 garlic cloves, finely chopped

2 slices bread, crusts removed

1 pound lean ground beef

1 cooked baby beet, chopped

pinch of paprika

2 teaspoons finely chopped fresh thyme

1 egg

Salt and pepper

Sprigs of fresh thyme, for garnish

Tomato relish

⅔ cup strained tomatoes

2 teaspoons creamed horseradish

Preheat the oven to 450°F.

To make the tomato relish, mix the strained tomatoes and creamed horseradish together in a small bowl. Cover and set aside until required.

Put the onion, garlic, and 2 teaspoons of water in a small pan and let simmer over low heat for 5 minutes. Increase the heat, bring to a boil, and cook until all the water has evaporated. Remove from the heat.

Meanwhile, tear the bread into pieces and place in a small bowl. Add enough cold water just to cover and let soak for 5 minutes. Squeeze the excess water from the bread and place in a bowl with the beef, onion and garlic mixture, beet, paprika, thyme, and egg. Season with salt and pepper to taste and mix thoroughly.

Form the mixture into 24 small balls between the palms of your hands. Thread 3 balls onto each of 8 metal skewers and place on a baking sheet. Bake in the preheated oven for 10 minutes, or until well browned. Transfer to a serving dish, garnish with a few sprigs of thyme, and serve with the tomato relish.

Chicken with Lime Stuffing

serves 4

1 whole chicken, weighing 5 pounds

oil, for brushing

1 large zucchini, grated

2 tablespoons butter

Juice of 1 lime

Lime slices and shreds of lime rind, for garnish

Stuffing

½ small zucchini, sliced

¾ cup lowfat cream cheese

Finely grated rind of 1 lime

2 tablespoons fresh breadcrumbs

Salt and pepper

Preheat the oven to 375°F.

To make the stuffing, trim and coarsely grate the zucchini and mix with the cheese, lime rind, breadcrumbs, and salt and pepper.

Carefully ease the skin away from the breast of the chicken with the fingertips, taking care not to split it.

Push the stuffing under the skin, to cover the breast evenly.

Place in a roasting pan, brush with oil, and roast for 20 minutes per 1 pounds plus 20 minutes, or until the chicken juices run clear when pierced with a skewer.

Meanwhile, trim the remaining zucchini and cut into long, thin strips with a vegetable peeler or sharp knife. Sauté in the butter and lime juice until just tender, then serve with the chicken. Garnish the chicken with the lime slices and shreds of lime rind and serve immediately.

Shrimp with Coconut Rice

serves 4

1 cup dried Chinese mushrooms
2 tablespoons vegetable or peanut oil
6 scallions, chopped
½ cup dry unsweetened shredded coconut
1 fresh green chile, seeded and chopped
1 cup jasmine rice
⅔ cup fish stock
1¾ cups coconut milk
12 ounces cooked shelled shrimp
6 sprigs fresh Thai basil

Place the mushrooms in a small bowl, cover with hot water, and set aside to soak for 30 minutes. Drain, then cut off and discard the stalks and slice the caps.

Heat the oil in a wok and stir-fry the scallions, coconut, and chile for 2–3 minutes,until lightly browned. Add the mushrooms and stir-fry for 3–4 minutes.

Add the rice and stir-fry for 2–3 minutes, then add the stock and bring to a boil. Reduce the heat and add the coconut milk. Let simmer for 10–15 minutes, until the rice is tender. Stir in the shrimp and basil, heat through, and serve.

Sloppy Joes

serves 1-6

1½ pounds lean ground beef
½ onion, diced
2 cloves garlic, minced
1 diced green bell pepper
2 cups water, divided
¾ cup ketchup
1½ tablespoons brown sugar
1 teaspoon Dijon mustard
Dash of Worcestershire sauce
1½ teaspoons salt, or to taste
½ teaspoon ground black pepper
Cayenne to taste
Hamburger buns

Place the ground beef and onions into a cold, large skillet and put over medium heat. Cook, stirring, until the beef begins to brown. As it cooks, break the meat into very small pieces with a spatula. The smaller the better.

Add the garlic and green pepper; cook stirring for 2 minutes. Add 1 cup of water. Bring to a simmer, scraping the bottom of the pan with a spatula to dissolve any browned bits.

Stir in the ketchup, brown sugar, mustard, Worcestershire, salt, pepper, and last cup of water. Bring to a simmer, reduce heat to low, and simmer for 30 to 45 minutes, or until most of the liquid has been evaporated, and the meat mixture is thick, rich and tender. Taste and adjust the seasoning. Serve hot on soft rolls.

Pork & White Wine Stew

serves 6

⅔ cup all-purpose flour
3 pounds pork tenderloin, cut into ¼-inch slices
4 tablespoons corn oil
2 onions, thinly sliced
2 garlic cloves, finely chopped
One 14.5 ounce can chopped tomatoes
1½ cups dry white wine
1 tablespoon torn fresh basil leaves
2 tablespoons chopped fresh parsley
Salt and pepper
Fresh oregano sprigs, to garnish
Fresh crusty bread, to serve

Spread the flour on a plate and season with salt and pepper. Coat the pork slices in the flour, shaking off any excess. Heat the oil in a flameproof casserole. Add the pork slices and cook over medium heat, turning occasionally, for 4–5 minutes, or until browned all over. Transfer the pork to a plate with a slotted spoon.

Add the onions to the casserole and cook over low heat, stirring occasionally, for 10 minutes, or until golden brown. Add the garlic and cook for an additional 2 minutes, then add the tomatoes, wine, and basil, and season to taste with salt and pepper. Cook, stirring frequently, for 3 minutes.

Return the pork to the casserole, cover, and simmer gently for 1 hour, or until the meat is tender. Add the parsley, garnish with oregano sprigs, and serve immediately with fresh crusty bread.

Corned Beef & Cabbage

serves 6-10

3½ to 5 pounds corned beef brisket

Spice packet from the corned beef package

2 teaspoons coarsely ground black pepper

1 bay leaf

Salt as needed

2 pounds white potatoes, cut in quarters

4 carrots, peeled, cut in chunks

1 onion, large dice

3 stalks celery, large dice

1 small green cabbage, cored, cut in 8 wedge

Place the corned beef, 1 teaspoon of the salt, pepper, and spices into a large pot along with 3 quarts of cold water. Cover and bring to a boil over high heat. Turn down the heat to low and slowly simmer for 2½ hours.

Add the potatoes, carrots, onions, and celery. Simmer, covered for 20 minutes. Add the cabbage and cook covered for another 20 minutes, or until the potatoes and vegetables are tender.

Remove the beef, and let rest 5 minutes. Slice against the grain and serve with the cabbage, potatoes, vegetables, and some of the cooking liquid. Serve with rye or dark bread and mustard on the side.

Pasta with Bacon & Tomatoes

serves 4

2 pounds small, sweet tomatoes
6 slices rindless smoked bacon
4 tablespoons butter
1 onion, chopped
1 garlic clove, crushed
4 sprigs fresh oregano, finely chopped
4 cups dried orecchiette
1 tablespoon olive oil
Salt and pepper
Freshly grated pecorino cheese, for serving

Blanch the tomatoes in boiling water. Drain, peel, and seed the tomatoes, then roughly chop the flesh.

Using a sharp knife, chop the bacon into small pieces.

Melt the butter in a pan. Add the bacon and fry until it is golden.

Add the onion and garlic and fry over medium heat for 5–7 minutes, until just softened.

Add the tomatoes and oregano to the pan and season with salt and pepper to taste. Reduce the heat and simmer for 10–12 minutes.

Bring a large pan of lightly salted water to a boil. Add the orecchiette and oil and cook for 12 minutes, until just tender, but still firm to the bite. Drain the pasta and transfer to a warmed serving dish or bowl.

Spoon the bacon and tomato sauce over the pasta, toss to coat, and serve with the cheese.

Potato, Leek & Chicken Pie

serves 4

8 ounces waxy potatoes, cubed
5 tablespoons butter
1 skinless chicken breast fillet, about 6 ounces, cubed
1 leek, sliced
2 cups sliced cremini mushrooms
2½ tablespoons all-purpose flour
1¼ cups milk
1 tablespoon Dijon mustard
2 tablespoons chopped fresh sage
One package (8 ounces) filo pastry, thawed, if frozen
3 tablespoons butter, melted
Salt and pepper

Preheat the oven to 350°F.

Bring a pan of lightly salted water to a boil and cook the potato cubes for 5 minutes. Drain and set aside.

Melt the butter in a skillet and cook the chicken cubes for 5 minutes or until browned all over.

Add the leek and mushrooms and cook for 3 minutes, stirring. Stir in the flour and cook for 1 minute, stirring continuously. Gradually stir in the milk and bring to a boil. Add the mustard, sage, and potato cubes and simmer for 10 minutes.

Meanwhile, line a deep pie dish with half of the sheets of filo pastry. Spoon the sauce into the dish and cover with 1 sheet of pastry. Brush the pastry with melted butter and lay another sheet on top. Brush this sheet with melted butter.

Cut the remaining filo pastry into strips and fold them onto the top of the pie to create a ruffled effect. Brush the strips with melted butter and cook for 45 minutes or until golden brown and crisp. Serve hot.

Layered Vegetable Casserole

serves 4

1 tablespoon olive oil, for brushing

1 pound 8 ounces potatoes

2 leeks

2 beefsteak tomatoes

8 fresh basil leaves

1 garlic clove, finely chopped

Salt and pepper

1¼ cups vegetable stock

Preheat the oven to 350°F. Brush a large flameproof dish with a little of the olive oil. Prepare all the vegetables. Peel and thinly slice the potatoes, trim and thinly slice the leeks, and slice the tomatoes.

Place a layer of potato slices in the bottom of the dish, sprinkle with half of the basil leaves and cover with a layer of leeks. Top with a layer of tomato slices. Repeat these layers until all the vegetables are used up, ending with a layer of potatoes. Stir the chopped garlic into the vegetable stock and season to taste with salt and pepper. Pour the stock over the vegetables and brush the top with the remaining olive oil.

Bake in the preheated oven for 1½ hours, or until the vegetables are tender and the topping is golden brown. Serve immediately.

Barbecued Baby Back Ribs

serves 6

2 full racks baby back pork ribs, trimmed of excess fat, patted dry

For the rub:

⅓ cup packed light brown sugar

3 tablespoons kosher salt

1 teaspoon ground black pepper

1 tablespoon smoked or regular paprika

½ teaspoon ground chipotle pepper

½ teaspoon dried thyme

½ teaspoon dried mustard

½ teaspoon garlic powder

½ teaspoon onion powder

¼ teaspoon cayenne pepper

1½ cups Kansas City style barbecue sauce

Pre-heat oven to 250°F.

Combine the spice rub ingredients in a small bowl and mix thoroughly. Place each rack of ribs in the center of its own large piece of heavy-duty aluminum foil. Generously apply the dry rub to each side of the two racks (more so on the meat side). Wrap each rack in foil; transfer to the refrigerator for at least 4 hours – overnight is even better.

Place the two foil-wrapped racks on a baking sheet and place in oven. Bake for 2 hours. Remove the ribs from oven, and using tongs, carefully open the foil (excess fat can be poured off). Place both racks on one piece of the foil, and brush barbecue sauce generously on both sides.

Increase the oven temperature to 350°F.

Return pan of ribs to the oven. Continue cooking, brushing on more barbecue sauce several times, until the ribs are fork tender and well glazed, about 30 to 45 minutes.

Remove and let rest for 5 minutes before cutting and serving. Ribs can be tossed in additional sauce if desired, and/or served with extra sauce on the side.

Firehouse Chili con Carne

serves 6

1 tablespoon vegetable oil

1 large yellow onion, diced

2½ pounds lean ground beef

3 cloves garlic, minced

¼ cup chile powder

1 tablespoon ground cumin

1 teaspoon freshly ground black pepper

½ teaspoon chipotle pepper

¼ teaspoon cayenne pepper

1 teaspoon dried oregano

1 teaspoon sugar

1 large green bell pepper, seeded and diced

1 large red bell pepper, seeded and diced

One 15-ounce can tomato sauce

2 tablespoons tomato paste

3 cups water, or more as needed

One 15-ounce can pinto beans, drained

One 15-ounce can kidney beans, drained,

Add the vegetable oil and onions to a Dutch oven, or other heavy pot. Place over medium-high heat and sauté for about 5 minutes, or until the onions begin to soften. Add the ground beef, and cook for about 10 minutes. As the beef browns, use a wooden spoon to break the meat into very small pieces.

Add the garlic, chili powder, ground cumin, black pepper, chipotle, cayenne, oregano, and sugar. Cook, stirring, for 2 minutes.

Stir in the bell peppers, tomato sauce, tomato paste, and water. Bring up to a simmer; reduce the heat to medium-low and cook, uncovered, stirring occasionally for 60 minutes.

After 60 minutes, stir in the beans and simmer for another 30 minutes. If needed, add more water anytime during the cooking to adjust desired thickness. Taste for salt and pepper, and adjust. Serve hot, garnished with sour cream, grated pepper jack, and fresh cilantro leaves.

Chicken Parmesan Casserole with Tomato Sauce

serves 6

6 boneless skinless chicken breasts (about 6 to 7 ounces each)
2 tablespoons olive oil
2 cloves garlic, minced
Hot red pepper flakes, to taste
4 cups marinara sauce
¼ cup chopped basil
1⅓ cup shredded mozzerella
⅔ cup grated Parmesan,
1 (5 ounce) package garlic croutons

For the sauce

¼ cup olive oil
1 onion, diced
1 rib celery, fine dice
4 cloves garlic, finely minced
1 teaspoon salt
2 teaspoons sugar
½ teaspoon dried Italian herbs
Pinch of red pepper flakes
1 teaspoon anchovy paste
1 teaspoon white wine vinegar
1 tablespoon tomato paste
Two 14.5 ounce cans plum tomatoes
2 tablespoons chopped fresh basil

Pre-heat oven to 350°F.

Place the chicken breasts on a plate and season both sides with salt and fresh ground black pepper. Set aside.

Spread the olive oil, garlic, and red pepper flakes evenly on the bottom of a 9 x 13 inch casserole dish. Add 1 cup of the marinara, and spread evenly. Place the chicken breasts in the dish, and space evenly so they cook uniformly. Top with the rest of the marinara sauce and basil.

Top with half the mozzerella, and half the Parmesan. Pour over the croutons and spread evenly. Top with the remaining cheese. Bake for 40 minutes, or until top is browned and the chicken is cooked through. Let rest for 5 minutes before serving with some sauce spooned from the bottom of the casserole.

For the sauce: In a saucepan, sweat the onions and celery in the olive oil for 5 to 6 minutes, or until they begin to turn translucent. Add the garlic and cook for 1 minute more. Add the salt, sugar, dried herbs, pepper flakes, anchovy paste, vinegar, and tomato paste. Cook, stirring, for 2 minutes.

Add the tomatoes, bring to a simmer, turn down to low and simmer gently, stirring occasionally for 45 minutes. Water may be added to adjust thickness. Taste and adjust seasoning and reserve until needed.

Prime Rib of Beef

serves 2 portions per rib

1 standing prime rib of beef roast (4 to 7 ribs, about 9 to 18 pounds), trimmed and tied

Room temperature butter, about ½ tablespoon per rib bone

Fresh coarse-ground black pepper, as needed

Kosher salt (or other larger grain, flake-style salt), as needed

2 tablespoons flour

4 cups cold beef broth, or veal stock if available

1 tablespoon fresh chopped tarragon, optional

For the sauce:

6 tablespoons creamed horseradish sauce
6 tablespoons sour cream

Pre-heat oven to 450°F.

Place the prime rib in a large, sturdy metal roasting pan. No rack is needed as bones form a natural rack. Rub the entire surface of the roast with butter, and season very generously with kosher salt and black pepper. Leave the prime rib out at room temperature for 2 hours.

When the oven is hot, put the roast in for 20 minutes to sear the outside. After 20 minutes turn the oven down to 325°F. and roast until the desired internal temperature is reached (see below). Some use 15 minutes per pound as a rule of thumb, but a good digital thermometer is a much better idea. The following are internal temperatures for removing the beef at, and not the final temperature. The meat will continue to cook after it's removed.

Rare: Remove at 110-115°F. (Final temp about 120-125°F.)

Medium-Rare: Remove at 120-125°F. (Final temp about 130-135°F.)

Medium: Remove at 130-135°F. (Final temp about 140-145°F.)

Transfer to a serving platter, and let the prime rib rest, loosely covered with foil, for at least 30 minutes before slicing and serving. Cutting into the meat too early will cause a loss of juice, and self-esteem.

For the sauce: In a small bowl mix the horseradish sauce and sour cream together.

Spaghetti & Meatballs

serves 24

2 tablespoons olive oil
1 yellow onion, diced fine
4 garlic cloves, minced
½ teaspoon dried Italian herbs
½ loaf day-old Italian bread, crust removed
¼ cup milk
2 pounds very cold ground beef
2 teaspoons salt
1 teaspoon freshly ground black pepper
2 large eggs, beaten
⅓ cup chopped fresh Italian parsley
¾ cup freshly grated Parmigiano-Reggiano cheese, plus more for service
6 cups marinara sauce, or other prepared pasta sauce
1 cup water
Thick spaghetti (allow 4 ounce uncooked per person), cooked according to directions

Pre-heat oven to 425°F.

Heat the olive oil in a saucepan over medium-low heat; add the onion, garlic, and a pinch of salt. Sweat for 6 to 7 minutes, or until soft and golden. Turn off heat, stir in the dried Italian herbs, let cool to room temperature.

Tear the bread into small chunks and place into a food processor (work in batches depending on the size of the machine). Pulse on and off to make fine breadcrumbs. You'll need 2 cups total. Add the crumbs to a bowl and toss with the milk to moisten. Let sit 10 minutes.

In a large mixing bowl, use your hands to combine the beef, salt, black pepper, eggs, parsley, cheese, breadcrumbs, and cooled onion mixture.

Wet your hands and roll golf ball-size meatballs; arrange on an oiled sheet pan. Bake 20 minutes. While the meatballs are browning in the oven, bring the pasta sauce and water to a simmer. When the meatballs are done, transfer into the hot sauce. Turn heat to very low, cover, and simmer gently for 45 minutes.

When they're done, cook the spaghetti, drain well (never rinse), and add to a large pasta bowl. Ladle some of the sauce from the meatballs over the pasta and toss to coat. Serve the spaghetti topped with the meatballs, sauce, and freshly grated cheese.

Pork Casserole

serves 6

¾ cup all-purpose flour

3 pounds pork tenderloin, cut into ¼-inch slices

4 tablespoons vegetable oil

2 onions, thinly sliced

2 garlic cloves, finely chopped

One 14.5 ounce can chopped tomatoes

1½ cups dry white wine

1 tablespoon torn fresh basil leaves

2 tablespoons chopped fresh parsley, plus extra sprigs to garnish

Salt and pepper

Fresh crusty bread, to serve

Spread the flour out on a plate and season to taste with salt and pepper. Toss the pork slices in the flour to coat, shaking off any excess. Heat the oil in an ovenproof casserole over medium heat. Add the pork slices and cook until browned all over. Using a slotted spoon, transfer the pork to a plate.

Add the onions to the casserole and cook over low heat, stirring occasionally, for 10 minutes, or until golden brown. Add the garlic and cook, stirring, for 2 minutes, then add the tomatoes with their juice, the wine, and basil leaves, and season to taste with salt and pepper. Cook, stirring frequently, for 3 minutes.

Return the pork to the casserole, cover, and simmer gently for 1 hour, or until the meat is tender. Stir in the chopped parsley. Serve immediately, garnished with parsley sprigs, and accompanied by fresh crusty bread.

Braised Lamb Shanks

serves 6

6 lamb shanks, about 5½ pounds-

2 tablespoons olive oil

½ teaspoon dried rosemary

½ teaspoon dried thyme

Salt and fresh ground black pepper to taste

1 tablespoon butter

1 onion, diced

1 rib celery, diced

1 large carrot, diced

1 tablespoon flour

4 cloves garlic, minced

½ cup red wine

1 cup chicken broth

1 tablespoon balsamic vinegar

½ cup water

Pinch cinnamon

1 teaspoon minced fresh rosemary leaves

Pre-heat oven to 450°F.

Place the shanks in a deep, 15 x 10 inch baking dish, or similar sized roasting pan, large enough to fit the shanks in one layer. Rub with the olive oil, dried rosemary and thyme. Season generously with salt and pepper on both sides. Roast for 30 minutes to brown the lamb.

While the lamb is browning, place a saucepan on medium-high heat, and add the butter. When the butter foams, add the onion, celery, and carrot. Cook for about 6 to 7 minutes, or until the vegetables soften and the edges start to brown and caramelize.

Stir in the flour and cook for 1 minute. Add the garlic and cook for 1 minute more. Stir in the wine. When the wine comes to a boil, stir in the chicken broth, balsamic vinegar, water, and cinnamon. Bring back to a boil, turn off and reserve.

When the lamb has finished browning, remove, and turn the oven down to 325°F. Pour over the sauce mixture, and distribute evenly. Cover with heavy-duty foil, crimping the edges to form a tight seal. Roast for 1 hour, lift the foil, turn over the shanks, rewrap and cook for 1 more hour, or until fork tender. Remove the lamb shanks to a large bowl, and cover with foil to keep warm. Pour the braising liquid into a saucepan, and boil on high. Roast in the oven for 20 minutes, or until the vegetables are almost tender. Remove and reserve. About 30 minutes before the beef is done, uncover and add the vegetables to the pot. Continue cooking until the beef and vegetables are tender.

Spicy Pork & Rice

serves 4

1¼ cups long-grain white rice
2½ cups cold water
12 ounces pork tenderloin
2 teaspoons Chinese five-spice powder
4 tablespoons cornstarch
3 large eggs, beaten
2 tablespoons brown sugar
2 tablespoons vegetable oil
1 onion, diced
2 cloves garlic, crushed
2 carrots, diced
1 red bell pepper, seeded and diced
1 cup peas
2 tablespoons butter
Salt

Rinse the rice under cold running water. Place the rice in a large pan, and add the cold water and a pinch of salt. Bring to a boil, cover, then reduce the heat and let simmer for about 9 minutes, or until all of the liquid has been absorbed and the rice is tender.

Meanwhile, slice the pork into very thin even-size pieces, using a sharp knife. Set the pork strips aside until required.

Whisk together the five-spice powder, cornstarch, 1 egg, and the sugar. Toss the pork in the mixture until coated.

Heat the oil in a large wok or skillet. Add the pork and cook over high heat until the pork is cooked through and crispy. Remove the pork from the wok with a slotted spoon and set aside until required.

Add the onion, garlic, carrots, bell pepper, and peas to the wok and stir-fry for 5 minutes.

Return the pork to the wok together with the cooked rice and stir-fry for 5 minutes.

Heat the butter in a skillet. Add the remaining beaten eggs and cook until set. Turn out onto a clean board and slice thinly. Toss the strips of egg into the rice mixture and serve immediately.

Creamy Pasta with Peas

serves 4

1 pound mixed plain and green dried taglatelli or spaghetti

¼ cup (½ stick) butter

6 cups fresh peas, shelled

¾ cup heavy cream

½ cup freshly grated romano cheese, plus extra for serving

Pinch of freshly grated nutmeg

Salt and pepper

Bring a large pan of lightly salted water to a boil. Add the pasta to the pan, bring back to a boil, and simmer for 8–10 minutes, until tender, but still firm to the bite.

Meanwhile, melt the butter in a heavy pan. Add the peas and cook over low heat, stirring frequently, for 4–5 minutes. Pour in ½ cup of the cream, bring to a boil, and simmer for 1 minute.

When the pasta is tender, but still has bite, drain well and add to the peas. Pour in the extra cream, add the romano cheese, and season with nutmeg and salt and pepper to taste. Toss well, then transfer to a warmed serving dish and serve immediately.

Chicken & Apple Casserole

serves 4

4 chicken portions, about 6 ounces each,
1 tablespoon olive oil
1 onion, chopped
2 celery stalks, coarsely chopped
1½ tablespoons all-purpose flour
1¼ cups clear apple juice
⅔ cup chicken stock
1 baking apple, cored and cut into quarters
2 bay leaves
1–2 teaspoons clear honey
1 yellow bell pepper, seeded and cut into chunks
1 tablespoon butter
1 large or 2 medium eating apples, cored and sliced
2 tablespoons brown sugar
Salt and pepper
1 tablespoon chopped fresh mint, to garnish

Preheat the oven to 375°F. Lightly rinse the chicken and pat dry with paper towels.

Heat the oil in a deep skillet and cook the chicken over medium–high heat, turning frequently, for 10 minutes, or until golden all over and sealed. Using a slotted spoon, transfer to an ovenproof casserole.

Add the onion and celery to the skillet and cook over medium heat, stirring frequently, for 5 minutes, or until softened. Sprinkle in the flour and cook, stirring constantly, for 2 minutes, then remove from the heat. Gradually stir in the apple juice and stock, then return to the heat and bring to a boil, stirring. Add the cooking apple, bay leaves, and honey and season to taste.

Pour over the chicken in the casserole dish, then cover and cook in the preheated oven for 25 minutes. Add the bell pepper and cook for an additional 10–15 minutes, or until the chicken is tender and the juices run clear when a skewer is inserted into the thickest part of the meat.

Meanwhile, preheat the broiler to high. Melt the butter in a pan over low heat. Line the broiler pan with kitchen foil. Brush the eating apple slices with half the butter, then sprinkle with a little sugar and cook under the broiler for 2–3 minutes, or until the sugar has caramelized. Turn the slices over. Brush with the remaining butter and sprinkle with the remaining sugar, and cook for an additional 2 minutes. Serve the stew garnished with the apple slices and mint.

Turkey Cutlets

serves 4-6

1½ cups all-purpose flour

1 teaspoon garlic powder

1 teaspoon onion powder

¼ teaspoon cayenne pepper

4 large eggs

4 cups Japanese-style panko breadcrumbs, or more as needed

2 pounds turkey cutlets, sliced or pounded to an even ¼ inch thickness

Salt and freshly ground black pepper to taste

1 teaspoon poultry seasoning

Canola oil for frying

Lemon wedges

Add the flour, garlic powder, onion powder, and cayenne into a shallow dish. Stir thoroughly to combine; reserve. Whisk the eggs in a mixing bowl; reserve. Pour the breadcrumbs into a shallow baking dish; reserve.

Season the turkey cutlets on both sides generously with the salt and freshly ground black pepper to taste, and dust lightly with the poultry seasoning.

Dredge the turkey cutlets in the seasoned flour. One or two at a time, dip the cutlets into the egg, and once coated, transfer into the breadcrumbs. Turn over several times, pressing lightly in the crumbs to make sure the meat is thoroughly coated. Transfer cutlets to a pan, and continue until they're all breaded. When done breading, let rest for 15 minutes before frying.

Pour about ¼ inch of oil into a large, heavy skillet (ideally cast iron) and set over medium high heat. When the oil is hot enough to fry (350°F. or test with a small piece of breading), cook for about 2 to 3 minutes per side, or until golden brown and cooked through.

Work in batches, drain on paper towels or wire rack, and keep in a warm oven (175°F.) until all are done. Serve immediately with lemon wedges, or other sauce of your choice.

Yankee Pot Roast

serves 8

Chuck roast, or any large (about 5 pounds)
Salt and fresh ground black pepper to taste
2 tablespoons vegetable oil
1 tablespoon butter
1 onion, diced
2 ribs celery, chopped
2 tablespoons flour
3 cloves garlic, minced
½ cup red wine
2 teaspoons tomato paste
2 cups chicken broth
1 bay leaf
1 teaspoon dried thyme
½ teaspoon salt
1½ pounds new potatoes
4 carrots, peeled, cut in large chunks
1 pound parsnips, peeled, cut in large chunks
1 tablespoon melted butter
2 tablespoons fresh chopped parsley

Pre-heat oven to 425°F. Generously season the beef with salt and fresh ground black pepper. Place a Dutch oven on a high heat on the stove, add the vegetable oil. When the oil is hot, brown the beef very well, about 5 minutes per side. Remove the meat to a platter, and turn the heat down to medium.

Add the butter, diced onions, celery, and a pinch of salt. Sauté for 5 minutes to brown, then add the flour. Add the garlic, cook, stirring, for 1 minute. Whisk in the wine, scraping to deglaze the browned bits from the bottom of the pot. Add the tomato paste, pour in the chicken broth.

Add the bay leaf, thyme, and salt. When the liquid comes to a simmer, stir well, and place the beef back into the pot. Turn the stove heat down to very low, and simmer gently for about 45 minutes per pound, or until fork tender. After 2 hours, carefully turn the beef over, cooking until done.

While the pot roast is cooking, prepare the vegetables. Add the potatoes, carrots, and parsnips to a roasting pan. Skim a tablespoon of beef fat from the surface of the beef's braising liquid. Drizzle it over the vegetables, along with the melted butter. Toss the vegetables to coat, and season. Roast in the oven for 20 minutes, or until the vegetables are almost tender. Remove and reserve. About 30 minutes before the beef is done, uncover and add the vegetables to the pot. Continue cooking until the beef and vegetables are tender.

Chicken and Sausage Gumbo

serves 6

⅓ cup vegetable oil
⅓ cup flour
1 onion, diced
3 ribs celery, large dice
2 green bell pepper, seeded, diced
½ cup minced green onions
3 cloves garlic, crushed fine
1 pound spicy, smoked sausage, cut in 1 inch pieces
6 cups chicken broth
One 10 ounce can diced tomatoes with green chilies
1½ pounds boneless, skinless chicken thighs, cut in 2 inch pieces
1 tablespoon Cajun seasoning
1 teaspoon salt
¼ teaspoon cayenne pepper, or to taste
½ teaspoon black pepper
2 cups frozen cut okra, thawed, drained
1 pound shrimp, peeled, deveined
Cooked white long grain rice, optional

To make the roux: In a heavy Dutch oven or pot, cook the oil and flour over medium low heat, stirring with a wooden spoon, until it's a light, nutty brown color.

Add the onion, celery, and bell pepper to the roux and cook for another 5 minutes to soften the vegetables. Add the green onions, garlic, and sausage; stir, and cook for 3 minutes.

Add the broth, tomatoes, chicken, Cajun seasoning, salt, cayenne pepper, and black pepper. Bring to a boil, reduce to low, and simmer, stirring occasionally, for 1 hour. Stir in the okra and simmer for another 30 minutes, or until the chicken is very tender.

Stir in the shrimp and cook for 3 to 4 minutes, or until they're cooked through. Taste for salt and spice, and adjust seasoning if needed. Serve hot with some cooked rice.

Stuffed Pork with Prosciutto

serves 4

1 pound 2-ounces piece of lean pork tenderloin

Small bunch fresh basil leaves

2 tablespoons freshly grated Parmesan cheese

2 tablespoons sun-dried tomato paste

6 thin slices prosciutto

1 tablespoon olive oil

Salt and pepper

Olive paste

⅔ cup pitted black olives

4 tablespoons olive oil

2 garlic cloves, peeled

Preheat the oven to 375°F.

Trim away the excess fat and membrane from the pork. Slice the pork lengthwise down the center, taking care not to cut all the way through.

Open out the pork and season the inside. Lay the basil leaves down the center. Mix the cheese and sun-dried tomato paste and spread over the basil.

Press the pork back together. Wrap the prosciutto around the pork, overlapping, to cover. Place on a rack in a roasting pan, seam side down, and brush with oil. Bake for 30–40 minutes, depending on thickness, until cooked through. Let stand for 10 minutes.

For the olive paste, place all the ingredients in a blender or food processor and blend until smooth. Alternatively, for a coarser paste, finely chop the olives and garlic and mix with the oil.

Drain the cooked pork, slice thinly, and serve with the olive paste.

Buttermilk Fried Chicken

serves 8

For the marinade

1 whole chicken (about 4 pounds), cut in 8 serving size pieces

1 teaspoon salt

1 teaspoon black pepper

1 teaspoon paprika

½ teaspoon cayenne pepper

½ teaspoon white pepper

1 teaspoon poultry seasoning

2 cups buttermilk

For the seasoned flour

2 cups all purpose flour

1 tablespoon salt

1 teaspoon black pepper

1 teaspoon paprika

pinch teaspoon cayenne pepper

½ teaspoon white pepper

1 teaspoon garlic salt

1 teaspoon onion powder

2 quarts peanut oil, or vegetable shortening for frying

Place the chicken in a large glass bowl or plastic container. Add all the seasonings, and toss to coat very thoroughly. Pour over the buttermilk. Use tongs to move the chicken pieces around until they are coated. Cover and refrigerate for 6 to 12 hours.

Mix together the seasoned flour ingredients in a large baking dish. Drain the chicken pieces in a colander, and toss into the flour. Toss to coat the chicken completely with the flour mixture. Make sure it's thoroughly covered, including all the nooks and crannies. Gently shake off excess flour, and reserve on a plate.

Heat the oil or shortening in a heavy Dutch oven to 350°F. Carefully add the chicken and fry for 10 minutes. Use tongs or a wire strainer to turn the pieces over, and continue cook for another 8 to 10 minutes approximately, or until crisp, golden brown, and you've reached an internal temperature of 175°F to 180°F.

Remove to drain on a wire rack for 5 minutes before serving. May be sprinkled with additional salt and/or hot pepper if desired.

Smothered Pork Chops

serves 4

4 large pork chops, about 1½ inch thick
1 teaspoon poultry seasoning
Salt and fresh ground black pepper to taste
2 tablespoons vegetable oil
1 tablespoon butter
1 large yellow onion, sliced
4 cloves garlic, finely minced
1 rounded tablespoon flour
1½ cups chicken broth
¼ cup buttermilk
¼ cup water
4 cups cooked rice, optional

Season pork chops on both sides with the poultry seasoning, salt and pepper. Heat the oil in a large frying pan over medium-high flame. When the oil is hot, brown the pork chops well, about 5 minutes per side. Remove from the pan and reserve on a plate.

Pour off the excess oil, and place the pan back on the stove over medium heat. Add the butter and the onions, along with a big pinch of salt. Sauté for about 10 minutes, or until the onions are well-browned. The onions need to caramelize for best results.

Stir in the garlic and cook for 1 minute. Stir in the flour and cook for 2 minutes. Add the chicken broth, buttermilk, and water. As the mixture comes to a simmer, use a wooden spoon to scrape any browned bits from the bottom of the pan.

Turn the heat to low, and let the onion gravy gently simmer for 15 minutes. Add a splash of water if it seems to be getting too thick. Add the pork chops and any juices back into the pan, and coat with the gravy. Cook for about 10 minutes, or until the pork reaches your desired level of doneness. Taste for seasoning and adjust if needed. Serve pork chops over rice, topped with the onion gravy.

Spicy Tomato Tagliatelle

serves 4

3 tablespoons butter
1 onion, finely chopped
1 garlic clove, crushed
2 small red chiles, seeded and diced
1 pound fresh tomatoes, peeled, seeded, and diced
¾ cup vegetable stock
2 tablespoons tomato paste
1 teaspoon sugar
1 pound 8 ounces fresh green and white tagliatelle
Salt and pepper

Melt the butter in a large pan. Add the onion and garlic and cook for 3–4 minutes or until softened.

Add the chiles to the pan and continue cooking for about 2 minutes.

Add the tomatoes and stock, reduce the heat, and let simmer for 10 minutes, stirring.

Pour the sauce into a food processor and blend for 1 minute until smooth. Alternatively, push the sauce through a strainer.

Return the sauce to the pan and add the tomato paste, sugar, and salt and pepper to taste. Gently reheat over low heat, until piping hot.

Bring a large pan of lightly salted water to a boil and cook the tagliatelle for 8–10 minutes or until tender, but still firm to the bite. Drain the tagliatelle, transfer to serving plates, and serve with the tomato sauce.

Pan-cooked Chicken

serves 4

4 chicken breasts, part boned

2 tablespoons butter

2 tablespoons olive oil

2 red onions, cut into wedges

2 tablespoons lemon juice

⅔ cup dry white wine

⅔ cup chicken stock

2 teaspoons all-purpose flour

One 14.5 ounce can artichoke halves, drained and halved

Salt and pepper

Chopped fresh parsley, for garnish

Season the chicken with salt and pepper to taste. Heat the oil and 1 tablespoon of the butter in a large skillet. Add the chicken and fry for 4–5 minutes on each side until lightly golden. Remove from the skillet using a slotted spoon.

Toss the onion in the lemon juice and add to the skillet. Gently fry, stirring, for 3–4 minutes until just beginning to soften.

Return the chicken to the skillet. Pour in the wine and stock, bring to a boil, cover, and simmer gently for 30 minutes.

Remove the chicken from the skillet, reserving the cooking juices, and keep warm. Bring the juices to a boil, and boil rapidly for 5 minutes.

Blend the remaining butter with the flour to form a paste. Reduce the juices to a simmer and spoon the paste into the skillet, stirring until thickened.

Adjust the seasoning according to taste, stir in the artichoke hearts, and cook for an additional 2 minutes. Pour the mixture over the chicken and garnish with the parsley.

Slow-Roasted Pulled Pork with Kansas City Barbecue Sauce

serves 6-8

3½ to 4 pounds pork shoulder roast, also called pork butt or Boston butt

1 tsp liquid smoke, optional

For the dry rub

2 tbsp brown sugar

1 tbsp salt

1 tbsp freshly ground black pepper

1 tbsp paprika

2 tsp chile powder

2 tsp garlic powder

2 tsp onion powder

2 tsp ground cumin

1 tsp cayenne pepper

For the sauce

2 cups ketchup

⅔ cup dark molasses

½ cup white vinegar

1 tsp paprika

1 tsp chili powder

1 tsp hot sauce

½ tsp freshly ground black pepper

½ tsp salt

½ tsp ground cinnamon

½ tsp ground allspice

½ tsp ground mace

½ tsp liquid smoke, optional

Pre-heat oven to 215°F.

Rinse the meat, and pat dry with paper towels. Trim off any large pieces of excess fat. Mix the rub ingredients together, and thoroughly coat all sides of the pork.

Place the pork, fattier side up, in a large Dutch oven. Pour ⅓ cup water into a small, ovenproof ramekin, and add the liquid smoke. Place this ramekin in the Dutch oven next to the meat. As the pork roasts, this will introduce moisture to the cooking environment, as well as add a subtle smokiness to the meat. Cover tightly with the lid, and place in the center of the preheated oven.

Roast pork for 12 hours, or until very fork tender. If you're using a thermometer, the internal temperature will be around 200°F. Turn off the oven and allow the pork to rest for 1 hour before removing

To serve, place the pork on a cutting board and use two forks to pull it apart into small pieces.

For the sauce: Whisk together the ingredients in a saucepan. Bring to a simmer over medium-low heat. Cook, stirring, for 3 minutes. Remove from heat, and let cool to room temperature before storing in an airtight container in the refrigerator. Served warm or room temperature as a condiment for grilled, roasted, and barbecued meats.

Braised Beef Short Ribs

serves 4

3½ pounds (8 pieces) beef short ribs
Salt and fresh ground black pepper as needed
4 slices bacon, cut in ½ inch pieces
1 large onion, diced
1 rib celery, diced
4 cloves garlic, minced
2 tablespoons flour
1 cup dry sherry wine
3 cups beef broth, or veal stock if available
6 springs fresh thyme
1 bay leaf
2 teaspoons tomato paste

Pre-heat oven to 350°F.

Add the bacon to a heavy Dutch oven and fry over a medium heat on the stove top until the fat is rendered out. Remove the bacon with a slotted spoon and reserve, leaving the fat in the pan.

Turn the stove heat up to medium-high, and brown the short ribs very well on all sides. Remove the short ribs and reserve. Add the onions and celery; reduce the heat to medium, and sauté for about 5 minutes, until the onions soften.

Add the garlic and flour; cook, stirring, for 2 minutes. Whisk in the sherry (by the way, don't even think of using cooking sherry); turn heat up to high, and bring to a boil, scraping off any browned bits. Add the beef broth, tomato paste, thyme, bay leaf, beef short ribs, and ½ teaspoon of salt.

When the liquid returns to a simmer, cover tightly, and place in the oven. Braise for 2 hours, or until the meat is fork tender. Skim any excess fat from the top. Taste and adjust the seasoning. Serve the short ribs with the sauce spooned over.

Stuffed Garlic Chicken

serves 4

4 part-boned chicken breasts

4 ounces frozen spinach, thawed

¾ cup lowfat ricotta cheese

2 garlic cloves, crushed

1 tablespoon olive oil

1 onion, chopped

1 red bell pepper, seeded and sliced

One 14.5 ounce can chopped tomatoes

6 tablespoons wine or chicken stock

10 stuffed olives, sliced

Salt and pepper

Sprigs of fresh flat-leaf parsley, for garnish

Pasta, for serving

Preheat the oven to 400°F.

Make a slit between the skin and meat on one side of each chicken breast. Lift the skin to form a pocket, being careful to leave the skin attached to the other side.

Put the spinach into a strainer and press out the water with a spoon. Mix with the ricotta, half the garlic, and the seasoning.

Spoon the spinach mixture under the skin of each chicken breast, then secure the edge of the skin with toothpicks.

Heat the oil in a skillet, add the onion, and cook for a minute, stirring. Add the remaining garlic and the bell pepper and cook for 2 minutes. Stir in the tomatoes, wine, olives, and seasoning. Set the sauce aside and chill the chicken if preparing in advance.

Bring the sauce to a boil, pour into an ovenproof dish, and arrange the chicken breasts on top in a single layer.

Cook, uncovered, for about 35 minutes, until the chicken is golden and cooked through. Test by making a slit in one of the chicken breasts with a skewer to make sure the juices run clear.

Spoon a little of the sauce over the chicken breasts, then transfer to serving plates, and garnish with the parsley. Serve with the pasta.

Beef & Vegetable Stew with Corn

serves 4

1 pound braising beef
1½ tablespoons all-purpose flour
1 teaspoon hot paprika
1–1½ teaspoons chili powder
1 teaspoon ground ginger
2 tablespoons olive oil
1 large onion, cut into chunks
3 garlic cloves, sliced
2 celery stalks, sliced
2 large carrots, chopped
1¼ cups lager
1¼ cups beef stock
3 cups potatoes, chopped
1 red bell pepper, seeded and chopped
2 corn cobs, halved
6 tomatoes, cut into quarters
1 cup shelled fresh or frozen peas
1 tablespoon chopped fresh cilantro
Salt and pepper

Trim any fat or gristle from the beef and cut into 1-inch chunks. Mix the flour and spices together. Toss the beef in the spiced flour until well coated.

Heat the oil in a large, heavy-bottom pan and cook the onion, garlic, and celery, stirring frequently, for 5 minutes, or until softened. Add the beef and cook over high heat, stirring frequently, for 3 minutes, or until browned on all sides and sealed.

Add the carrots, then remove from the heat. Gradually stir in the lager and stock, then return to the heat and bring to a boil, stirring. Reduce the heat, then cover and simmer, stirring occasionally, for 1½ hours.

Add the potatoes to the pan and simmer for an additional 15 minutes. Add the red bell pepper and corn cobs and simmer for 15 minutes, then add the tomatoes and peas and simmer for an additional 10 minutes, or until the beef and vegetables are tender. Season to taste with salt and pepper, then stir in the cilantro and serve.

Chicken & Rice Casserole

serves 4

⅔ cup long-grain rice

1 tablespoon dry sherry

2 tablespoons light soy sauce

2 tablespoons dark soy sauce

2 teaspoons dark brown sugar

1 teaspoon salt

1 teaspoon sesame oil

2 pounds skinless, boneless chicken meat, diced

4 cups chicken stock

⅓ cup sliced mushrooms

⅓ cup water chestnuts, halved

1 cup broccoli florets

1 yellow bell pepper, sliced

4 teaspoons grated fresh gingerroot

Whole chives, for garnish

Cook the rice in a pan of boiling water for 15 minutes. Drain well, rinse under cold water, and drain again thoroughly.

Mix together the sherry, soy sauces, sugar, salt, and sesame oil.

Stir the chicken into the soy mixture, turning to coat well. Let marinate for about 30 minutes.

Bring the stock to a boil in a pan or preheated wok. Add the chicken with the marinade, mushrooms, water chestnuts, broccoli, bell pepper, and ginger.

Stir in the rice, reduce the heat, cover, and cook for 25–30 minutes, until the chicken and vegetables are cooked through. Transfer to serving plates, garnish with the chives, and serve.

Lamb Pot Roast

serves 4

One 3-4 pounds leg of lamb

Salt and freshly ground pepper, to taste

3–4 sprigs of fresh rosemary

6 bacon slices

4 tablespoons olive oil

2–3 garlic cloves, crushed

2 onions, sliced

2 carrots, sliced

2 celery ribs, sliced

1¼ cups dry white wine

1 tablespoon tomato paste

1¼ cups lamb or beef stock

2-3 tomatoes, peeled, cut into quarters, and seeded

1 tablespoon chopped fresh parsley

1 tablespoon chopped fresh oregano or marjoram

Sprigs of fresh rosemary, for garnish

Preheat oven to 350°F.

Season the lamb. Lay the sprigs of rosemary over the lamb, cover evenly with the bacon slices, and tie in place with string. Heat the oil in a large skillet and fry the lamb for about 10 minutes, turning several times. Remove the lamb from the skillet, and set aside.

Transfer the oil from the skillet to a large ovenproof casserole and cook the garlic and onion for 3–4 minutes until they begin to soften. Add the carrots and celery and cook for a few minutes longer.

Lay the lamb on top of the vegetables and press down to partly submerge the meat. Pour the wine over the lamb, add the tomato paste, and let simmer for about 3–4 minutes. Add the stock, tomatoes, and herbs and season with salt and pepper to taste. Bring back to a boil for an additional 3–4 minutes.

Cover the casserole tightly and cook in a moderate oven for 2–2 ½ hours until the lamb is very tender.

Remove the lamb from the casserole and, if preferred, take off the bacon and herbs along with the string. Keep warm. Strain the juices, skimming off any excess fat, and serve in a pitcher. Arrange the vegetables around the lamb, or serve them in a separate dish. Garnish the lamb with the sprigs of rosemary.

Pot-roast Pork

serves 4

1 tablespoon vegetable oil
4 tablespoons butter
2 pounds 4 ounces boned and rolled pork loin
4 shallots, chopped
2 fresh thyme sprigs, plus extra to garnish
⅔ cup cider
⅔ cup chicken stock or water
8 celery stalks, chopped
2 tablespoons all-purpose flour
⅔ cup heavy cream
Salt and pepper
Freshly cooked peas, to serve

Heat the oil with half the butter in a heavy bottom pan or flameproof casserole. Add the pork and cook over medium heat, turning frequently, for 5–10 minutes, or until browned. Transfer to a plate.

Add the shallots to the pan and cook, stirring frequently, for 5 minutes, or until softened. Add the thyme sprigs and return the pork to the pan, with any juices that have collected on the plate. Pour in the cider and stock, season to taste with salt and pepper, then cover and simmer for 30 minutes. Turn the pork over and add the celery. Re-cover the pan and cook for an additional 40 minutes.

Meanwhile, make a paste by mashing the remaining butter with the flour in a small bowl. Transfer the pork and celery to a platter with a slotted spoon and keep warm. Remove and discard thyme. Whisk the paste, a little at a time, into the simmering cooking liquid. Cook, stirring constantly, for 2 minutes, then stir in the cream and bring to a boil.

Slice the pork and spoon a little of the sauce over it. Garnish with thyme sprigs and serve immediately with the celery, peas, and remaining sauce.

Chicken & Fall Vegetable Casserole

serves 4

3 tablespoons olive oil

2 leeks, sliced

2 garlic cloves, sliced

2 large chicken breasts, about 6 ounces each, cut into bite-size pieces

2 sweet potatoes, peeled and cut into chunks

2 parsnips, scrubbed and sliced

1 red bell pepper, seeded and cut into strips

1 yellow bell pepper, seeded and cut into strips

1½ cups mixed wild mushrooms, cleaned

2¼ cups coarsely chopped tomatoes

4 cups cooked white long-grain rice

1 small bunch fresh parsley, chopped

1 cup grated sharp cheddar cheese

Salt and pepper

Preheat the oven to 350°F.

Heat the oil in a large skillet over medium heat, then add the leeks and garlic and cook, stirring frequently, for 3–4 minutes, or until softened.

Add the chicken and cook, stirring frequently, for 5 minutes. Add the sweet potatoes and parsnips and cook, stirring frequently, for 5 minutes, or until golden and beginning to soften. Add the bell peppers and mushrooms and cook, stirring frequently, for 5 minutes.

Stir in the tomatoes, rice, and parsley and season to taste with salt and pepper.

Spoon the mixture into an ovenproof dish. Scatter over the cheddar cheese and bake in the preheated oven for 20–25 minutes. Serve immediately.

Chicken Fried Steak With Country Cream Gravy

serves 4

4 6-ounce beef cube steaks

Salt and freshly ground black pepper to taste

1 cup all-purpose flour

1 tablespoon paprika

½ teaspoon white pepper

2 eggs, beaten

¼ cup milk

Vegetable oil as needed

For the gravy...

4 ounces ground pork sausage, or pork sausage link with casing removed

3 green onions, light parts chopped, green parts sliced and reserved

3 tablespoons butter

¼ cup all-purpose flour

2½ cups cold milk

Salt and freshly ground black pepper to taste

Pinch of cayenne

Season both sides of the steaks generously with salt and pepper.

Whisk together the eggs and milk in a pie pan and reserve. Add the flour, paprika, and white pepper into a second pie pan, and mix well to combine.

One at a time, dip the cube steaks into the egg mixture, turning to coat completely, and then dredge in the flour, coating both sides. Place the egged and floured steaks on a plate, and allow to rest for 10 minutes.

Add about a ¼ inch of vegetable oil to a large skillet, and place over medium-high heat. When the oil begins to shimmer, add the steaks and cook about 3 to 4 minutes per side, until golden brown and cooked through. Remove and drain for a couple minutes on a wire rack set over some paper towels. If working in batches, keep the cooked steaks in a warm oven until the rest are done.

Gravy: Lightly brown the sausage in a medium saucepan over medium heat. As it cooks, break the meat up into very small pieces with a wooden spoon. Add the light parts of the green onion and the butter; sauté for a few minutes, until the onions are translucent.

Stir in the flour and cook this pasty mixture for 3 minutes. Whisk in the cold milk gradually until combined. The gravy will thicken as it comes up to a simmer. When it simmers, reduce the heat to low and cook, stirring occasionally, for 15 minutes. Before serving, season with salt, pepper, and cayenne to taste.

4

Grandma's Bake Sale

Creamy Coffee Cake

serves 8-10

Butter, for greasing
1 cup self-rising flour
¼ teaspoon baking powder
4 tablespoons unsweetened cocoa
7 tablespoons sugar
2 eggs
2 tablespoons light corn syrup
⅔ cup vegetable oil
⅔ cup milk

Filling

1 teaspoon instant coffee
1 tablespoon boiling water
1¼ cups heavy cream
2 tablespoons confectioners' sugar

For decorating

2 ounces grated chocolate
Confectioners' sugar, to dust

Preheat oven to 350°F.

Lightly grease 6 x 2-inch cake pans.

Sift the flour, baking powder, and unsweetened cocoa into a large mixing bowl. Stir in the sugar. Make a well in the center and stir in the eggs, syrup, oil, and milk. Beat with a wooden spoon, gradually mixing in the dry ingredients to make a smooth batter. Divide the mixture among the prepared pans.

Bake for 35–45 minutes, or until springy to the touch. Let stand in the pans for 5 minutes, then turn out onto a cooling rack to cool completely.

Dissolve the instant coffee in the boiling water and place in a bowl with the cream and confectioners' sugar. Whip until the cream is just holding its shape. Use half of the cream to sandwich the 3 cakes together. Spread the remaining cream over the top and sides of the cake. Lightly press the grated chocolate into the cream around the edge of the cake.

Transfer to a serving plate. Dust lightly with the confectioners' sugar, carefully remove the parchment paper, and serve.

Butter Shortbread Wedges

makes 8

½ cup (1 stick) butter, softened

3 tablespoons sugar

2 tablespoons confectioners' sugar

2 cups all-purpose flour

Pinch of salt

2 teaspoons orange flower water or grated orange rind

Preheat the oven to 300°F.

Lightly grease an 8-inch shallow round cake pan.

In a large mixing bowl, cream together the butter, the granulated sugar, and the confectioners' sugar until light and fluffy.

Sift the flour and salt into the creamed mixture. Add the orange flower water and bring everything together to form a soft dough.

On a lightly floured surface, roll out the dough to an 8- inch round and place in the pan. Mark out 8 evenly-spaced lines on the dough for cutting into wedges when cooked.

Bake for 30–35 minutes or until the cookie is pale golden and crisp.

Let the shortbread cool before removing the wedges from the pan. Store in an airtight container.

Double Fudge Brownies

makes 9

8 ounces bittersweet baking chocolate, broken or chopped into small pieces
5 tablespoons butter, sliced into pieces
1 cup sugar
¼ teaspoon salt
2 tablespoons water
2 large eggs
1 teaspoon vanilla extract
¾ cup all-purpose flour
½ cup chopped walnuts (optional)

Pre-heat oven to 325°F.

Place the chocolate, butter, sugar, salt, and water in small saucepan over a very low flame. Heat, stirring often, until the chocolate and butter are melted.

Pour into a mixing bowl. Stir in the eggs, one at a time. Stir in the vanilla. Stir in the flour. Stir in the nuts, if using.

Pour into a lightly greased 8 inch-square baking dish.

Bake for 35 minutes. Cool completely before cutting into 9 squares.

Chocolate & Orange Ring

serves 8

¾ cup (1½ cups) butter, softened, plus extra for greasing
¾ cup sugar
3 eggs, beaten
1¼ cups self-rising flour, sifted
¼ cup unsweetened cocoa, sifted
5–6 tablespoons orange juice
Grated rind of 1 orange

Preheat the oven to 350°F.

Lightly grease a 10-inch Bundt pan mold.

In a mixing bowl, cream together the butter and sugar with an electric whisk for about 5 minutes.

Add the beaten egg a little at a time, whisking well after each addition.

Using a metal spoon, fold the flour into the creamed mixture carefully, then spoon half the mixture into a separate mixing bowl.

Fold the unsweetened cocoa and half the orange juice into one bowl and mix gently. Fold the orange rind and remaining orange juice into the other bowl and mix gently.

Place spoonfuls of each of the mixtures alternately into the mold, then drag a skewer through the mixture to create a marbled effect.

Bake in a preheated oven, 350°F, for 30–35 minutes, or until well risen and a skewer inserted into the center comes out clean.

Let the cake cool in the mold before turning out carefully onto a cooling rack.

Molasses Oat Squares

makes 21

1 cup (2 sticks) butter
1 cup light molasses sugar
½ cup light corn syrup
4½ cups rolled oats

Preheat the oven to 350°F. Line a 9-inch square cake pan with parchment paper.

Put the butter, sugar, and syrup into a pan and heat over low heat for 2–3 minutes until melted. Mix in the rolled oats and stir well.

Pour the mixture into the prepared pan, press down well, and bake in the center of the preheated oven for 30–35 minutes until golden brown but still moist and slightly soft when pressed.

Remove from the oven and let cool for 5 minutes. Cut into 21 squares and let cool completely for about 30 minutes in the pan.

Carefully remove the squares from the pan and store in an airtight container in a cool place for up to 3–4 days.

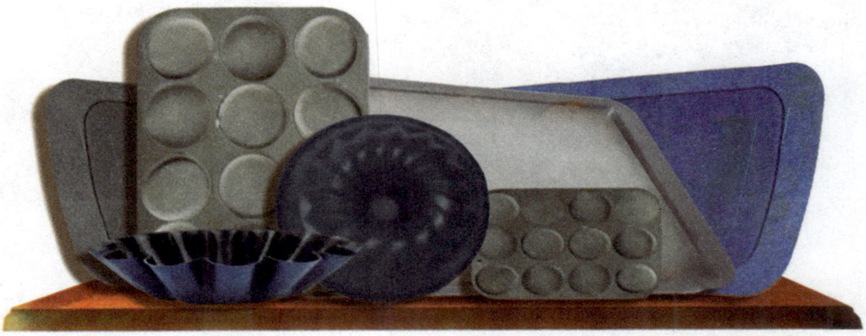

Cherry Pie

serves 8

Pie Crust

1 cup all-purpose flour

¼ teaspoon baking powder

½ teaspoon allspice

½ teaspoon salt

¼ cup sugar

4 tablespoons unsalted butter

1 egg, beaten, plus extra for glazing

Filling

4 cups pitted fresh cherries or drained canned cherries

½ cup sugar

½ teaspoon almond extract

2 teaspoons cherry brandy

¼ teaspoon allspice

2 tablespoons cornstarch

2 tablespoons water

2 tablespoons unsalted butter

Preheat the oven to 425°F. Grease a 9-inch round tart pan.

To make the pie crusts, sift the flour and baking powder into a large bowl. Stir in the allspice, salt, and sugar. Rub in the butter with your fingertips until the mixture resembles fine breadcrumbs. Add the beaten egg and mix to a firm dough. Cut the dough in half and roll each half into a ball. Roll out one half of the dough and line the pan.

To make the filling, put half of the cherries and the sugar in a large saucepan. Bring to a simmer over low heat, stirring, until the sugar has dissolved. Stir in the almond extract, brandy, and allspice. In a separate bowl, mix the cornstarch and water to form a paste. Remove the saucepan from the heat, stir in the cornstarch paste, then return to the heat and stir continuously until the mixture boils . Stir in the remaining cherries, pour into the pastry shell.

Cut the remaining dough into long strips about ½ inch wide. Lay five strips evenly across the top of the filling. Now lay six strips crosswise over the strips, folding back every other strip each time you add another crosswise strip, to form a lattice. Trim off the ends and seal the edges with water. Use your fingers to crimp around the rim, then brush the top with beaten egg to glaze.

Cover with foil and bake for 30 minutes. Discard the foil, then bake for an additional 15 minutes, or until the crust is golden.

Blackberry & Apple Cake

serves 10

1 tablespoon butter, for greasing

2 large baking apples (2 cups) peeled and diced

3 tablespoons lemon juice

2 cups whole wheat flour

2½ teaspoons baking powder

1 teaspoon ground cinnamon, plus extra for dusting

1 cup blackberries, thawed if frozen, plus extra, for decorating

1 cup firmly packed light brown sugar

1 egg, beaten lightly

¾ cup lowfat plain yogurt

¼ cup white or brown sugar

One small sliced apple, for decorating

Preheat oven to 375°F.

Grease a 9 x 5 x 3-inch loaf pan with a little butter and line with parchment paper. Core, peel, and finely dice the cooking apples. Place them in a pan with the lemon juice, bring to a boil, cover, and simmer for 10 minutes, until soft. Beat well. Set aside to cool.

Sift the flour, baking powder, and cinnamon into a bowl, adding any bran that remains in the sifter. Stir in ⅔ cup of the blackberries and the sugar.

Make a well in the center of the ingredients and add the egg, yogurt, and cooled apple paste. Mix until thoroughly blended. Spoon the mixture into the prepared loaf pan and level over the top with a spatula.

Sprinkle with the remaining blackberries, pressing them down into the cake batter, and top the batter with the crushed sugar lumps. Bake in a preheated oven, 375°F for 40–45 minutes, then let cool in the pan.

Turn the cake out and peel away the parchment paper. Serve dusted with cinnamon and decorated with the blackberries and apple slices.

Almond Cookies

makes 32

1 cup butter (2 sticks), softened

1 cup unblanched almonds

6 tablespoons confectioners' sugar, plus extra for sifting

2 cups all-purpose flour

2 teaspoons vanilla extract

½ teaspoon almond extract

Preheat oven to 350°F.

Line 2 cookie sheets with wax paper. Using a cook's knife, finely chop the almonds, or process them in a small food processor, taking care not to overprocess them into a paste. Set aside.

Put the butter in a bowl and beat with an electric mixer until smooth. Sift in the confectioners' sugar and continue beating until creamed and smooth.

Sift in the flour from above the bowl and beat it in until blended. Add the vanilla and almond extracts and beat a gain to form a soft dough. Stir in the chopped almonds.

Using a teaspoon, shape the dough into 32 round balls about the size of walnuts. Place on the prepared cookie sheets, spacing them apart. Bake in a preheated oven, for 20–25 minutes until set and just starting to turn golden brown.

Let the cookies stand on the cookie sheets for 2 minutes to firm up. Sift a thick layer of confectioners' sugar over them. Transfer to a cooling rack and let cool completely.

Lightly dust with more confectioners' sugar, just before serving. Store the cookies in an airtight container for up to a week.

Pecan Pie

serves 8

For the pie dough

1¾ cups all-purpose flour, plus extra for dusting

½ cup (1 stick) butter

2 tablespoons white sugar

For the filling

5 tablespoons butter

½ cup light brown sugar

⅔ cup dark corn syrup

2 extra-large eggs, beaten

1 teaspoon vanilla extract

1 cup pecans

Pre-heat oven to 400°F.

For the pie dough, place the flour in a bowl and rub in the butter using your fingertips until it resembles fine breadcrumbs. Stir in the granulated white sugar and add enough cold water to mix to a firm dough. Wrap in plastic wrap and chill for 15 minutes, until firm enough to roll out.

Roll out the dough on a lightly-floured counter and use to line a 9 inch round, loose-bottomed tart pan. Prick the bottom with a fork. Chill for 15 minutes.

Place the tart pan on a cookie sheet, line with a sheet of parchment paper, and fill with dried beans. Bake in the pre-heated oven for 10 minutes. Remove the paper and beans and bake for an additional 5 minutes. Reduce the oven temperature to 350°F.

For the filling, place the butter, brown sugar, and corn syrup in a saucepan and heat gently until melted. Remove from the heat and quickly beat in the eggs and vanilla extract.

Coarsely chop the pecans and stir into the mixture. Pour into the tart shell and bake for 35 to 40 minutes, until the filling is just set. Serve warm or cold.

Whoopie Pies

serves 8-10

2 cups all-purpose flour

3 tablespoons unsweetened cocoa powder

½ teaspoon baking soda

¼ teaspoon salt

1 stick (½ cup) unsalted butter, softened

1 cup packed brown sugar

1 large egg

1¼ teaspoons vanilla

½ cup buttermilk

For the filling

4 ounces softened cream cheese

1 (7 ounce) jar marshmallow creme

Pre-heat oven to 375°F.

Add the flour, cocoa powder, baking soda and salt to a mixing bowl. Stir the mixture with a whisk to combine and aerate. Reserve until needed.

Add the butter and brown sugar to a large mixing bowl, and beat with an electric mixer until light and fluffy. Beat in the egg and vanilla until thoroughly combined.

Add a third of the flour mixture; stir until combined. Add half the buttermilk; stir until combined. Add half the remaining flour; stir until combined. Add the remaining buttermilk, stir in, and finally mix in the last of the flour.

Line two heavy-duty baking sheets with silicon baking mats or parchment paper. Spoon the batter on the baking sheets, forming rounds about ½ inch high and 3 inches wide. You should fit about 8 per pan. As long as the batter is spooned on about ½ inch thick, you can really make these as small or large as you like.

Bake for 12 to 14 minutes, or until the tops look cooked, and are slightly firm to the touch. Remove and let rest for 15 minutes on the baking sheets. Remove to racks and let cool completely before filling.

In a mixing bowl beat the cream cheese until light and fluffy. Use a spatula to fold in the marshmallow creme. Spread a couple spoons of filling on the flat side of one of the cakes, and top with another to form a sandwich.

New York Cheesecake with Fruit Sauce

serves 8-10

½ cup (1 stick) butter
1¾ cups finely crushed grahams crackers
1 tablespoon sugar
2 pounds cream cheese
1¼ cups sugar
2 tablespoons all purpose flour
1 teaspoon vanilla extract
Finely grated zest of 1 orange
Finely grated zest of 1 lemon
3 eggs
2 egg yolks
1¼ cups heavy cream

For the sauce

1 cup berries, such as blackberries or raspberries
2 tablespoons water
2 to 3 tablespoons granulated white sugar
2 tablespoons fruit liqueur, such as crème de cassis or crème de framboise

Pre-heat the oven to 350°F.

Place a small saucepan over low heat, melt the butter and remove from heat. Stir in crushed crackers and the 1 tablespoon sugar. Mix. Press the cracker mixture into bottom of a 9 inch cake pan. Place in an oven and bake for 10 minutes. Remove and cool.

Increase oven temperature to 400°F.

With an electric food mixer beat cream cheese until creamy and gradually add sugar and flour and beat until smooth. Beat in the vanilla extract, orange and lemon zest, then one at a time beat in the eggs and egg yolks. Finally beat in the cream. The mixture should be light and whippy.

Grease the sides of the cake pan and pour in the filling. Transfer to the pre-heated oven and bake for 15 minutes. Reduce heat to 200°F. and bake for an additional 30 minutes. Turn the oven off and leave to cool for 2 hours. Cover and refrigerate overnight.

For the sauce: Put all the ingredients into a small, heavy-bottomed pan and heat gently, until the sugar has dissolved and the fruit juices run. Process to a paste in a food processor, then push through a non-metallic strainer into a serving bowl to remove the seeds. Add more sugar if necessary and serve warm or cold.

Chocolate Chip Cookies

makes 30

2¼ cups all-purpose flour

1 teaspoon baking soda

1 teaspoon salt

1 cup butter (2 sticks), room temperature

¾ cup packed light brown sugar

¾ cup white sugar

1 teaspoon vanilla extract

2 large eggs

2 cups dark or semi-sweet chocolate chips

1 cup chopped walnuts, optional

Pre-heat oven to 375°F.

Add the flour, baking soda and salt to a small mixing bowl. Whisk together briefly to combine. In another bowl, use an electric mixer to beat the butter, brown sugar, white granulated sugar, and vanilla extract until light and creamy.

Add eggs one at a time, beating thoroughly after each addition. Stir in the flour mixture until combined. Stir in the chocolate chips and nuts, if using. Drop the cookie dough by rounded tablespoons on un-greased cookie sheets about 3 inches apart.

Bake for about 10 minutes, or until lightly browned around the edges. Let sit on the baking sheets for 2 minutes, and then remove to wire cooling racks.

Carrot Cake with Cream Cheese Frosting

serves 8

2 cups all-purpose flour
1 teaspoon salt
2 teaspoons baking powder
1 teaspoon baking soda
2 teaspoons cinnamon
½ teaspoon ground ginger
2 cups sugar
1¼ cups vegetable oil
4 large eggs
¼ cup melted butter
2 cups raw grated carrots
One 8 ounce can crushed pineapple, drained
½ cup chopped pecans
½ cup chopped walnuts

For the frosting

½ cup (1 stick) unsalted butter, softened
8 ounces (1 cup) cream cheese, softened
1 tablespoon milk
1 teaspoon vanilla
1 pound powdered sugar

Pre-heat oven to 350°F.

Whisk together the flour, salt, baking powder, baking soda, cinnamon, and ginger in a mixing bowl for a minute or two; reserve until needed.

In another mixing bowl, combine the sugar, oil, and eggs. Whisk until thoroughly combined. Whisk in the melted butter. Use a spatula to stir in the carrots, pineapple, and nuts. Stir in the flour mixture in two additions.

Scrape the batter into a lightly greased 13 x 9 inch dish. Bake for about 40 minutes, or until the top springs back slightly when gently touched with your finger. Remove and allow to cool completely before frosting.

To make the frosting: Use an electric mixer to beat together the butter, cream cheese, milk, and vanilla until light and fluffy. Gradually beat in the powdered sugar to form a smooth frosting. Spread evenly over the cooled cake.

Spiced Apple Ring

serves 8

- **¾ cup (1½ sticks) butter, softened, plus extra for greasing**
- **¾ cup sugar**
- **3 eggs, lightly beaten**
- **1¼ cups self-rising flour**
- **1 teaspoon ground cinnamon**
- **1 teaspoon ground allspice**
- **2 apples, cored and grated**
- **2 tablespoons apple juice or milk**
- **¼ cup slivered almonds**

Preheat the oven to 350°F.

Lightly grease a 10-inch ovenproof ring mold.

In a mixing bowl, cream together the butter and sugar until light and fluffy. Gradually add the beaten eggs, beating well after each addition.

Sift the flour and spices, then carefully fold them into the creamed mixture with a figure-eight movement.

Stir in the grated apples and the apple juice or milk and mix to a soft dropping consistency.

Sprinkle the slivered almonds around the base of the mold and spoon the cake mixture on top. Level the surface with the back of the spoon.

Bake for about 30 minutes until well risen and a fine skewer inserted into the center comes out clean.

Let the cake cool in the pan before turning out and transferring to a cooling rack to cool completely. Serve the apple ring cut into slices.

Chocolate Caramel Squares

makes 9

½ cup (1 stick) butter, cut into small pieces, plus extra for greasing

1½ cups all-purpose flour

3 tablespoons soft brown sugar, sifted

Topping

3 tablespoons butter, softened

3 tablespoons light brown sugar

1¾ cups canned condensed milk

¾ cup milk chocolate pieces

Preheat the oven to 375°F.

Grease a 9 x 9 x 1½-inch square cake pan.

Sift the flour into a mixing bowl and rub in the butter with your fingers until the mixture resembles fine breadcrumbs. Add the sugar and mix to form a firm dough.

Press the dough into the bottom of the prepared pan and prick all over with a fork.

Bake for 20 minutes, or until lightly golden. Let cool in the pan.

To make the topping, place the butter, sugar, and condensed milk in a nonstick pan and cook over gentle heat, stirring continuously, until the mixture comes to a boil.

Reduce the heat and cook for 4–5 minutes until the caramel is pale golden and thick and is coming away from the sides of the pan. Pour the topping over the shortbread base and let cool.

When the caramel topping is firm, melt the milk chocolate in a heatproof bowl set over a pan of simmering water. Spread the melted chocolate over the topping, let it set in a cool place, then cut the shortbread into squares to serve.

Peanut Butter Cookies

makes 12-15

1½ cups all-purpose flour

½ teaspoon baking powder

½ teaspoon salt

1 cup creamy peanut butter

½ cup butter, room temperature

1¼ teaspoons vanilla extract

½ cup firmly packed brown sugar

½ cup white sugar

2 eggs

Pre-heat oven to 350°F.

Sift together the flour, baking powder, and salt in a mixing bowl; reserve. In a large mixing bowl, cream the peanut butter, butter, and vanilla together until smooth. Add the sugars, and cream for one more minute. Mix in the eggs one at a time. Mix in the flour, half at a time.

Wrap the dough in plastic wrap and refrigerate for at least 2 hours. Once chilled, roll or scoop the dough into 1½ inch balls, and place 3 inches apart on an ungreased or silicon-lined baking sheet.

Use a fork to flatten each ball by making a crisscross pattern. Bake for 15 minutes or until golden. Remove cookies from oven, and let cool on the baking sheet for 5 minutes. Transfer to a cooling rack with a spatula, and allow to cool to at least warm before enjoying.

Sweet Potato Pie

serves 8-10

For the pie dough

1¼ cups all-purpose flour, plus extra for dusting

½ teaspoon salt

¼ teaspoon sugar

1½ tablespoons butter, diced

3 tablespoons vegetable shortening, diced

2 to 2½ tablespoons ice-cold water

For the filling

1 pound orange-fleshed sweet potatoes,

3 extra-large eggs, beaten

½ cup packed brown sugar

1½ cups canned evaporated milk

3 tablespoons butter, melted

2 teaspoons vanilla extract

1 teaspoon ground cinnamon

1 teaspoon ground nutmeg or freshly grated nutmeg

½ teaspoon salt

Pre-heat oven to 425°F.

To make the pie dough, sift the flour, salt, and sugar into a bowl. Add the butter and vegetable shortening to the bowl and rub in with the fingertips until fine crumbs form. Sprinkle over 2 tablespoons of the water and mix with a fork until a soft dough forms. Add ½ tablespoon of water if the dough is too dry. Wrap in plastic wrap and chill for at least 1 hour.

Meanwhile, bring a large pan of water to a boil over high heat. Add the sweet potatoes and cook for 15 minutes. Drain, then cool them under cold running water. When cool, peel, then mash. Put the sweet potatoes into a separate bowl and beat in the eggs and sugar until very smooth. Beat in the remaining ingredients, except the whipped cream, then set aside until required.

Roll out the dough on a lightly floured counter into a thin 11 inch circle and use to line a 9 inch pie plate, about 1½ inches high. Trim off the excess dough and press the floured tines of a fork around the edge. Prick the base of the pastry shell all over with the fork and place crumpled kitchen foil in the center. Bake in the oven for 12 minutes, or until lightly golden.

Remove the pastry shell from the oven, take out the foil, pour the filling into the shell, and return to the oven for an additional 10 minutes. Reduce the oven temperature to 325°F and bake for a further 35 minutes, or until a knife inserted into the center comes out clean.

Rich Apple Biscuits

makes 8

½ cup (1 stick) butter, cut into small pieces, plus extra for greasing

2 cups self-rising flour

1 tablespoon sugar

pinch of salt

1 apple, peeled, cored, and chopped

1 egg, beaten

2 tablespoons molasses

5 tablespoons milk

Preheat the oven to 425°F

Lightly grease a baking sheet.

Sift the flour, sugar, and salt into a mixing bowl.

Rub in the butter with your fingertips until the mixture resembles fine breadcrumbs.

Stir the chopped apple into the mixture until combined.

Mix together the beaten egg, molasses, and milk. Add to the dry ingredients to form a soft dough.

On a lightly floured kitchen counter, roll out the dough to a thickness of ¾ inch and cut out 8 biscuits, using a 2-inch plain pastry cutter.

Arrange the biscuits on the baking sheet and bake for 8–10 minutes.

Transfer the biscuits to a cooling rack and cool slightly before serving. Serve the biscuits split in half and spread with butter.

Marbled Pound Cake

serves 8-10

Batter

¼ cup semisweet chocolate pieces

3 tablespoons whole milk

5 tablespoons butter

½ cup sugar

1 egg, beaten

3 tablespoons sour cream

1 cup self-rising flour

½ teaspoon baking powder

½ teaspoon vanilla extract

Preheat the oven to 325°F

Grease a 9 x 5 x 3-inch loaf pan and line with parchment paper.

Melt the chocolate, place it in a small heatproof bowl with the milk, and set the bowl over a saucepan of simmering water. Heat gently until just melted. Remove from the heat.

Cream together the butter and sugar until light and fluffy. Beat in the egg and sour cream. Sift the flour and baking powder over the mixture, then fold in using a metal spoon.

Spoon half the batter into a separate bowl and stir in the chocolate mixture. Add the vanilla extract to the plain batter.

Spoon the chocolate and vanilla batters alternately into the prepared loaf pan, swirling lightly with a knife for a marbled effect. Bake for 40–45 minutes, or until well risen and a toothpick when inserted comes out clean.

Cool in the pan for 10 minutes, then turn out and finish cooling on a wire rack.

Checkerboard Cookies

makes 18

¾ cup (1½ sticks) butter, softened, plus extra for greasing

½ cup confectioners' sugar

1 teaspoon vanilla extract or grated rind of ½ orange

2¼ cups all-purpose flour

2 ounces semisweet chocolate

A little beaten egg white

Preheat the oven to 350°.

Lightly grease a baking sheet. Beat the butter and confectioners' sugar in a mixing bowl until light and fluffy. Beat in the vanilla extract.

Gradually beat in the flour to form a soft dough. Use your fingers to incorporate the last of the flour and bring the dough together.

Melt the chocolate. Divide the dough in half and beat the melted chocolate into one half. Keeping each half of the dough separate, cover and let chill for 30 minutes.

Roll out each piece of dough to a rectangle measuring 3 x 8 inches long and 1½ inches thick. Brush one piece of dough with a little egg white and place the other on top.

Cut the block of dough in half lengthwise and turn over one half. Brush the side of one strip with egg white and butt the other up to it, so that it resembles a checkerboard.

Cut the block into thin slices and place each slice flat on the prepared cookie sheet, allowing enough room for the slices to spread out a little during cooking.

Bake in a preheated oven, 350°F° for about 10 minutes, until just firm. Let cool on the cookie sheets for a few minutes, before carefully transferring to a cooling rack with a spatula. Let cool completely.

Chocolate Marshmallow Cake

serves 6

6 tablespoons unsalted butter

1 cup sugar

½ teaspoon vanilla extract

2 eggs, beaten lightly

½ cup semisweet chocolate, broken into pieces

⅔ cup buttermilk

1¼ cups self-rising flour

½ teaspoon baking soda

pinch of salt

¼ cup grated milk chocolate, for decorating

Frosting

6 ounces (¾ cup) white marshmallows

1 tablespoon milk

2 egg whites

2 tablespoons sugar

Preheat the oven to 325°F.

Grease a 6 x 2-inch round cake pan and line with parchment paper. Cream the butter, sugar, and vanilla together in a bowl until pale and fluffy, then gradually beat in the eggs.

Melt the semisweet chocolate in a heatproof bowl over a pan of simmering water. When the chocolate has melted, stir in the buttermilk gradually, until well combined. Remove the pan from the heat and cool slightly.

Sift the flour, baking soda, and salt into a separate bowl.

Add the chocolate mixture and the flour mixture alternately with the creamed mixture, a little at a time. Spoon the mixture into the ovenproof bowl and smooth the surface. Bake for 50 minutes until a toothpick inserted into the center of the cake comes out clean. Turn out onto a cooling rack to cool.

Meanwhile, make the frosting. Put the marshmallows and milk in a small pan and heat very gently until the marshmallows have melted. Remove the pan from the heat and set aside to cool before spreading on the cake.

Sticky Pecan Pie Bars

makes 10 bars

Crust

2 tablespoons butter

1¼ cups all-purpose flour

¼ cup firmly packed light brown sugar

Topping

2 large eggs

6 tablespoons melted butter

½ cup firmly packed light brown sugar

⅓ cup chopped pecans

½ cup dark corn syrup

½ teaspoon vanilla extract

Preheat the oven to 375°F.

Line a shallow 9-inch square baking pan with parchment paper and grease the papers.

Place 2 tablespoons of the butter in a saucepan and heat gently until melted. Let cool slightly.

Place the flour and remaining butter, cut into cubes, in a large bowl and rub the butter in with your fingertips until the mixture resembles fine breadcrumbs. Stir in ¼ cup of the sugar, then spoon the mixture into the pan and press down firmly with the back of a spoon. Bake in the preheated oven for 20 minutes.

Meanwhile, place the eggs in a large bowl and beat lightly. Add the remaining sugar, the pecans, melted butter, dark corn syrup, and vanilla extract and stir together until combined.

Pour the mixture over the crust in the pan and bake in the oven for an additional 15–20 minutes, or until firm to the touch and golden brown. Remove from the pan and let cool. When cold, cut into 10 bars to serve.

Sugared Lemon Cookies

makes 50

½ cup (1 stick) butter, softened, plus extra for greasing
½ cup sugar
grated rind of 1 lemon
1 egg, beaten
4 tablespoons lemon juice
3 cups all-purpose flour
1 teaspoon baking powder
1 tablespoon milk
Confectioners' sugar, for dredging

Preheat oven to 325°.

Lightly grease several baking sheets.

In a mixing bowl, cream together the butter, sugar, and lemon rind until pale and fluffy.

Add the beaten egg and lemon juice a little at a time, beating well after each addition.

Sift the flour and baking powder into the creamed mixture and blend together. Add the milk, mixing to form a soft dough.

Turn the dough out onto a lightly floured counter and divide into about 50 equal-size pieces.

Roll each piece into a sausage shape with your hands and twist in the middle to make an "S" shape.

Place on the prepared baking sheets and bake for 20 minutes. Let cool completely on a cooling rack. Dredge with the confectioners' sugar to serve.

White Chocolate Cakes

makes 18

½ cup (1 stick) butter softened, plus extra for greasing

7 tablespoons sugar

2 eggs, lightly beaten

1¼ cups self-rising flour

2 tablespoons milk

½ cup semisweet chocolate chips

¼ cup unsweetened cocoa

Frosting

1 cup white chocolate

6 ounces (¾ cup) lowfat soft cheese

Preheat oven to 350°F.

Lightly grease an 18-cup muffin pan.

Beat together the butter and sugar until pale and fluffy. Gradually add the eggs, beating well after each addition. Add a little of the flour if the mixture begins to curdle. Add the milk, then fold in the chocolate chips.

Sift together the remaining flour and unsweetened cocoa and fold into the mixture with a metal spoon or spatula. Divide the mixture equally among the cups and level the tops.

Bake in a preheated oven, for 20 minutes, or until well risen and springy to the touch. Let cool on a cooling rack.

To make the frosting, melt the chocolate, then let cool slightly. Beat the cream cheese until softened slightly, then beat in the melted chocolate. Spread a little of the frosting over each cake and chill for 1 hour before serving.

Cinnamon Swirl Sour Cream Bundt Cake

serves 6-8

2½ cups all-purpose flour
1 teaspoon baking powder
1 teaspoon baking soda
½ teaspoon salt
¾ cup (1½ sticks) unsalted butter
1½ cups sugar
3 large eggs
1 cup sour cream
1 teaspoon vanilla extract
½ cup chopped walnuts, optional

For the swirl
1 tablespoon ground cinnamon
3 tablespoons brown sugar
2 tablespoons sugar

For the glaze
1 cup powdered sugar
About 1½ tablespoons milk
1 teaspoon ground cinnamon, or to taste

Pre-heat oven to 350°F.

Whisk together the flour, baking powder, baking soda, and salt in a mixing bowl for a minute; reserve until needed.

Cream the butter and sugar together until light and fluffy. Beat in the eggs one at a time, mixing thoroughly before adding the next. Beat in the sour cream and vanilla until combined. Add the flour mixture, stirring just until combined. Stir in the walnuts.

Butter a 10 inch bundt pan, and lightly dust with flour. Pour half the batter into the pan and spread evenly. Mix the ingredients for the swirl in a small bowl. Sprinkle evenly around the center of the batter. Cover with the rest of the batter.

Bake for 50 minutes, or until a toothpick inserted in the center comes out clean. Let cool 20 minutes before removing from the pan.

For the glaze: Add the powdered sugar to a small mixing bowl, stir in enough milk to create a thick, but pourable glaze. Stir in the cinnamon to taste. Drizzle over the top of the cake. Once the icing is set, slice and serve with lots of hot coffee.

Apple & Cinnamon Bars

makes 14 bars

Crust

½ cup (1 stick) unsalted butter

⅔ cup sugar

1 teaspoon vanilla extract

2 eggs, beaten

1 cup flour

2 large apples peeled, cored, and diced

2 tablespoons lemon juice

Topping

⅓ cup finely chopped, blanched almonds

¼ cup all-purpose flour

¼ cup firmly packed light brown sugar

½ teaspoon ground cinnamon

2 tablespoons unsalted butter, melted

Preheat the oven to 350°F

Grease and line a 11 x 7-inch cake pan.

Cream together the butter, sugar, and vanilla extract until pale. Gradually add the eggs, beating thoroughly.
Sift in the flour and fold in evenly.

Prepare the apples by peeling, dicing and sprinkling with lemon juice. Add to the flour mixture and mix.

Spread the mixture into the bottom of the cake pan. Pat the mixture down with the back of a wooden spoon or spatula.

For the topping, mix all the ingredients to a crumbly texture and sprinkle over the cake. Bake the cake in the preheated oven for 45–55 minutes, unti firm and golden.

Cut into bars and serve warm or cooled.

Pound Cake with Orange Glaze

serves 6

2 cups all-purpose flour
1 teaspoon baking powder
¼ teaspoon baking soda
½ teaspoon salt
2 sticks (1 cup) unsalted butter
1¼ cups white sugar
1 tablespoon grated lemon zest
1 tablespoon grated orange zest
4 eggs
½ cup buttermilk

For the glaze

1 cup confectioner's sugar
1½ tablespoons fresh orange juice, or as needed
1 tablespoon freshly grated orange zest

Pre-heat oven to 325°F.

Butter one 8 x 4 inch loaf pan, and dust with flour. Set aside.

Sift together the flour, baking powder, baking soda, and salt in a mixing bowl. Set aside.

In a large mixing bowl, use an electric mixer to beat the butter, sugar, and zests until very light and creamy. Beat in the eggs, one at time, beating very thoroughly after each addition. Use a spatula to mix in flour alternately with the buttermilk, ending with flour. Scrape the batter into the prepared loaf pan.

Bake for 1 hour to 1 hour 15 minutes, or until a toothpick inserted in the center comes out clean. Remove and let rest for 15 minutes, then turn onto a cooling rack. Let cool 15 more minutes before glazing.

Stir together the orange glaze ingredients, adding enough orange juice to get a smooth spreadable consistency. Apply to the top of the warm cake. Let the pound cake cool completely before slicing.

Fruit Crumble Tart

serves 8

Dough

1¼ cups all-purpose flour, plus extra, for dusting

2 tablespoons sugar

½ cup (1 stick) butter, diced

1 tablespoon water

Filling

1½ cups raspberries

2 cups plums, halved, pitted, and coarsely chopped

3 tablespoons firmly packed light brown sugar

Topping

1 cup all-purpose flour

⅓ cup firmly packed light brown sugar

4 tablespoons butter, diced

⅔ cup chopped mixed nuts

1 teaspoon ground cinnamon

Cream or ice cream, for serving

Preheat the oven to 400°F.

To make the dough, place the flour, sugar, and butter in a bowl and rub in the butter with your fingertips. Add the water and bring together with your fingers to form a soft dough. Wrap in plastic wrap and chill in the refrigerator for 30 minutes.

Roll out the dough on a lightly floured counter and use it to line the base of a 9 x 3-inch loose-bottom tart pan. Prick the base of the tart shell with a fork and chill in the refrigerator for about 30 minutes.

To make the filling, toss the raspberries and plums together with the sugar and spoon into the tart shell.

To make the crumble topping, combine the flour, sugar, and butter in a bowl. Rub in the butter with your fingertips until the mixture resembles coarse breadcrumbs. Stir in the nuts and ground cinnamon.

Sprinkle the crumble topping over the fruit and press down gently with the back of a spoon. Bake for 20–25 minutes, until the topping has turned golden brown. Serve with cream or ice cream.

Chocolate & Apricot Squares

makes 9 squares

½ cup (1 stick) butter, plus extra for greasing
¾ cup white chocolates pieces
4 eggs
½ cup sugar
1¾ cups all-purpose flour
1 teaspoon baking powder
Pinch of salt
½ cup dried apricots, chopped

Preheat the oven to 350°F.

Lightly grease a 9 x 9 x 1½-inch square cake pan and line the bottom with parchment paper.

Melt the butter and chocolate in a heatproof bowl set over a pan of simmering water. Stir frequently with a wooden spoon until the mixture is smooth and glossy. Let the chocolate mixture cool slightly.

Beat the eggs and sugar into the butter and chocolate mixture until well combined.

Fold in the flour, baking powder, salt, and chopped dried apricots, and mix together well.

Pour the mixture into the pan and bake for 25–30 minutes.

The center of the cake may not be completely firm when you take it out of the oven, but it will set as it cools. Let it cool in the pan.

When the cake is completely cold turn it out of the pan and carefully slice into squares to serve.

Black and White Brownies

makes 24 bars

½ cup (1 stick) butter

2 cups semisweet chocolate pieces

For the cream cheese mix

6 tablespoons butter

8 ounces cream cheese

¾ cups sugar

3 eggs

3 tablespoons flour

1 tablespoon vanilla extract

For the chocolate mix

6 eggs

2¼ cups sugar

1½ cups flour

1½ teaspoons baking powder

1½ teaspoons salt

1½ tablespoons vanilla extract

1 teaspoon almond extract

Preheat oven to 350°F. Slowly melt the butter and the chocolate in a glass bowl placed over a pan of gently simmering water. Mix well and set aside to cool.

With a whip attachment make the cream cheese mix. Cream the butter, then add the cream cheese and sugar, and beat until fluffy. Add in the eggs, then the flour, and the vanilla extract.

In a separate bowl make the chocolate mix. Whip the eggs and sugar until fluffy. Stir together the flour, baking powder, salt, and mix into egg mixture. Finally mix in the melted chocolate and butter, and the vanilla and almond extract.

In a 9 x 13-inch pan, lined with parchment, spread half the chocolate mixture. Spread the cream cheese layer over that to cover, then spoon the remaining chocolate batter on the top. Swirl the mixture with a knife to create a marbled effect.

Bake for 40 minutes. Cool and cut into bars.

Chocolate Butter Cake

serves 8–10

2 tablespoons butter, melted, plus extra for greasing

4 eggs

½ cup sugar

1 cup all-purpose flour

1 tablespoon unsweetened cocoa

¼ cup semisweet chocolate chips melted

1¼ cups finely chopped walnuts

Frosting

¼ cup semisweet chocolate chips

½ cup (1 stick) butter

1¼ cups confectioners' sugar

2 tablespoons whole milk

Walnut halves, for decorating

Preheat the oven to 325°F.

Grease a 6 x 2-inch deep round cake pan and line with parchment paper.

Place the eggs and sugar in a mixing bowl and whisk with electric beaters for 10 minutes, or until the mixture is light and foamy and the whisk leaves a trail that lasts a few seconds when lifted.

Sift together the flour and unsweetened cocoa and fold in with a metal spoon or spatula. Fold in the melted butter, the chocolate, and the chopped walnuts.

Pour into the prepared pan and bake for 30–35 minutes, or until springy to the touch.

Let cool in the pan for 5 minutes, then transfer to a cooling rack to cool completely. Cut the cold cake into 2 layers.

To make the frosting, melt the chocolate and let cool slightly. Beat together the butter, confectioners' sugar, and milk in a bowl until the mixture is pale and fluffy. Whisk in the melted chocolate.

Sandwich the 2 cake layers with some of the frosting and place on a serving plate. Spread the remaining frosting over the top of the cake with a spatula, swirling it slightly as you do so.

Decorate the cake with the walnut halves and serve.

Fruit Loaf

makes 1 loaf

Corn oil, for brushing
2 cups rolled oats
½ cup firmly packed light brown sugar
1 teaspoon ground cinnamon
¾ cup golden raisins
1 cup seedless raisins
2 tablespoons malt extract
1¼ cups unsweetened apple juice
1 cup self-rising whole wheat flour
1½ teaspoon baking powder

Preheat the oven to 350°F

Grease a 9 x 5 x 3-inch loaf pan and line with parchment paper.

Place the oats, sugar, cinnamon, golden raisins, raisins, and malt extract in a bowl. Pour in the apple juice, stir well, and let soak for 30 minutes.

Sift the flour and baking powder into the mixture.

Spoon the mixture into the prepared pan and bake in the preheated oven for 1½ hours, or until firm and a toothpick inserted into the center comes out clean.

Let cool in the pan for 10 minutes, then turn out onto a cooling rack and let cool.

Index